After I came back from Monte Cassino in VE year (June 1985), with the old soldiers, families and friends, I started to think about how to put this book together.

My father, like others of that generation, was called up and sent abroad to defend freedom. I thought the best way to tell his story was to take the reader through time: 1914-1948, using diaries newspaper reports and information that was available to the public during this period.

John A.Walker
cosmos-original-productions.co.uk

Photograph of Sergeant Jiggy, with his mother and father and brother (on the back cover) was taken while on Embarkation leave.

And ye shall hear of wars and rumours of wars: see that ye be not troubled: for these things must come to pass, but the end is not yet. (Matthew24:6)

The Pop Festival
Silent Faces at the Races
The Film Festival
Music-lovers
Art-lovers
Lucy Lovelock
The Zephyrman
Poems for the 21 Century

CD Albums:
The Silent Scene
In the Light
Beyond the Controller's Reach

Published by
cosmos-original-productions.co.uk
(check website for availability)

SERGEANT JIGGY

A True Story

John A.Walker

C
www.cosmos-original-productions.co.uk

Sergeant Jiggy
a cosmos original
isbn: 0-9534703-1-8

Set in Garamond.
published by
Cosmos Original Productions, Glasgow.

Printed and bound in Great Britain by
4edge Ltd, Hockley. www.4edge.co.uk

To the memory
of
Johnny and Georgina

1

As was his duty to God and man, the first minister of Greenbank church, the reverent James Fraser, one Sunday in February 1915, lifted up his hand and welcomed another child into the Christian faith. He christened him George Armstrong Walker, and as he held the child in his arms the baby's blue eyes looked around the church in a pure state of wonder.

Clarkston Toll, where the child had been born a few months ago, came under the parish of Cathcart. The area lay about five and a half miles from the city centre of Glasgow. Records show that in 1841, 330 people were recorded to have lived here, and in 1891 this had increased to 825.

Many people who now lived on the south side of Glasgow knew that the Celts, the Danes, and the Saxons had been here at one time: for you could still see traces of them in the faces of the local people. However, no one was sure where the name Clarkston originated from. Could it have been a town full of clerks in the Middle Ages? No one seemed to know.

After the baptism the proud parents returned to their home just down the road from the church. Their attractive stone built tenement flat, situated behind an arch, had been named after someone called Rowallandale. The tenement flat had a pub, a cafe, and a small group of shops opposite it at the toll. Rent was £8 a year.

Clarkston, like all communities in Scotland at this time, had its own identity. They had a cartwright, a blacksmith, a grocer, a publican, a draughtsman, a horse-shoer, a fishmonger, a draper, a jeweller, and on the right-hand side of the road going back up towards the church, Mr Tom Lindsay, a canny man, had turned his house into an artist's studio, and from there he sold his art. Although everyone loved his paintings he knew that he had also to make a living, so to help him do this he invested in the new wonder of the day: photography.

George a year or two later was taken up to his house and, as was the fashion of the day, he stood on a chair and got his picture taken.

Georgina, the boy's mother, born 31st August in the year 1892, as a young lady had come to this area a few years ago to work for a man named Vost. The Vost family were well-to-do people who lived half way down the Eastwood Mains Road, on the left-hand side going towards Giffnock. There she learned all the crafts of a maid: cooking, cleaning, and looking after babies.

Georgina originated from the borders, a place west of the old Middle March called Langholm. All the guide books at this time declared that Langholm had one of the prettiest landscapes in the country, neither wide, nor grand, but lovely.

She hailed from a famous border clan. In fact the name Armstrong was so famous in Scottish history that some people thought they had come over to this country with the Duke of Normandy in 1066.

As regards the written word, the first reported mention of the name Armstrong is chronicled in 1235: an Armstrong appears to have been pardoned at Carlisle for killing someone. She may have been gentle, but the clan were a tough lot indeed: *Invictus Maneo*.

The Armstrong clan, legend has it, even prevented the Romans at one time from occupying Scotland. Many historians thought their name came from the French family Fortinbras: strong in the arm.

Other historians - as ever with academics there was another school of thought - felt that the Armstrong name came via a Danish connection from Northumberland.

After everything had been considered by the scholars of the day it seemed that the Armstrong name, like so many other things in life, could not be pinned down. To put it in context truth had once again outwitted history and myth indisputable fact.

Johnny, the boy's father, born on the 27th July 1884, hailed from Newton Mearns. The Mearns, situated not all that faraway from Clarkston Toll, is higher up and further away from Glasgow than the Toll. They say a castle was built in the Mearns, by Roland de Merns in the 12th century, and on top of it another one in the 15th century. Mary Queen of Scots is said to have stayed there. The Mearns, like most Scottish towns around this time, relied upon sheep and cattle for its living. The town was certainly well-known in days gone by, when horse-drawn carriages stopped outside the Malletsheugh Inn on their way up and down to London.

Johnny did not have the romance through a name - like his wife - that went all the way back to the 12th century. However, his cousin had a grocer's shop on the right-hand side of the cross, and his mother, who liked a nip of whisky and a little bit of snuff - old though she was - would sometimes go there during the day.

His mother stayed at number 32 Main Street; she had once worked at the Calico Printers just round the corner. The lacemaking firm where she had ironed sheets had premises on the Barrhead Road. There they made table-covers, bed-sheets, and other things. Cotton calico, printing and dyeing was the dominant industry in Britain at this time. Everyone called her granny Bowman; she was born in the year 1859: a time of great expectations, Gladstone, Disraeli, the British in India and all that.

Johnny and Georgina had not long moved into their house at Clarkston Toll, when Britain declared war on Germany. Citizens were soon urged to do their duty to God and their country. The morning paper on the day of the birth, 9 December 1914, tried to advance the cause before the slaughter as best it could, so that men from all walks of life would flock to the colours: 'All War is Good. But this is the Best of All.'

There were plenty of volunteers and when some of the Busby and Clarkston soldiers came back from the war in the spring of 1915, on furlough, the local paper commented on how the locals thought the military training had smartened them up. One old man aged seventy from Clarkston around this time complained about being too old to fight. He told the local newspaper the Southern Press: 'I want to have a go at the German Hun!'

All the Newspapers by the beginning of the new year were well into the conflict; for it was going to be the war to end all wars, with rifles, tanks, zeppelins, and poison gas. At the end of 1914, the Daily Mirror printed a monster Christmas magazine packed full of the most controversial photographs. They obviously wanted to show the readers what war was really like - just in case they could not imagine it.

There had not been a war between two great powers in Europe since 1876; the diplomats had done their job. At this time in Great Britain only men had the right to change things with a vote, and it was the same all over Europe, only Finland and Norway had women in politics.

The world some said, by 1915, had been growing unstable for many a long year, and some men who studied history declared that new countries like Germany and Italy were living on their nerves. The workers reckoned it had a lot to do with capitalism: for capitalism created unemployment, and unemployment created poverty, and poverty created wars. The industrial magnets, on the other hand, blamed socialism; for socialism they said meant Marxism, and Marxism meant a class struggle. So Marxism became for educated people the antithesis of capitalism. Although it is fair to say that in Britain by 1915, you could still join a union and not be part of an extreme group; however there was no use thinking or worrying too much about these kinds of things now, for Britain was at war again and man, eternal man, was heading for destruction. There were around 400 million souls living in Europe at this time, and the average age that a fellow could expect to live to, according to one egghead, was about 46.

The war had shut the mills at Langholm and Georgina's sister, who George soon tenderly called aunty Bell - for she was married now - came to work at Weir Pumps at Cathcart. She stayed with them at Rowallandale for a time during the Great War while her husband Matt went to fight in France.

It is true to say that by February 1915, many men had read Lord Kitchener's famous recruitment poster: 'YOUR COUNTRY NEEDS YOU,' went to war, and just disappeared. On the other hand it is also true to say that many new faces appeared behind stonewalls - just like George's. Yes, the world during the first year of the war still seemed to be set on an advanced course, strange though that may sound.

Mr Allan, the owner of the property at Rowallandale, and Donald Adair, the cartwright, like all the other men around the town, worked every day except Sunday.

During the day Georgina would take her son George outside, and they would sometimes wander across the road in the direction of the cafe, where Mr and Mrs Tomasso worked. There were a few shops there, and one outlet was very important indeed: the sweetie shop. The trade in this area was slow, but it was sure trade. There may have been a war on, but people just tried to get on with things as best they could. Sometimes Georgina would watch the world go by, mainly men dressed in dark suits and coats and fashionable women in

Jaunty new hats, and it was natural for her to wonder what sort of world her son would grow up in. Life for mother and son seemed strange and wonderful at this point in time. There had been talk before the war of the tramcar coming out to Clarkston from Cathcart, but no one was sure of anything anymore.

A few years later another great event took place inside Rowallandale, and George was told about it. His mother came up to him and declared that he now had a little friend to play with. And as she showed him the baby boy, she said proudly, "Look you have a brother."

Presently, George's brother was christened John at Greenbank church by Mr Fraser, just like George had been 14 months ago.

As soon as Maisy Craig, whose dad had the grocers shop nearby, heard the news she came round to help, and thereafter she kept in touch with the family. A few years later Maisy took George and John for walks up the Mearns Road, and on summer days they all picked bluebells and other flowers for mum.

When the time came for her son, George, to enrol for school Georgina took him up the road to Busby Primary, and just for good measure she brought along his younger brother, John, just to show him what it was all about.

They all set out early in the morning and walked up the hill from Clarkston Toll, past the Sheddens. Then they turned right at the Bull Road and, when they got to the first group of houses, they walked up as far as the stonewall until the country seemed to disappear.

The school at Busby, set around houses, bushes and trees, may have had a football park beside it, but it still seemed a queer place for a young boy to go to so early in the morning. And when George was told that he had to go and join the other boys and girls, who were all running around the playground in front of the cold dark grey building, suddenly he felt the world change and he started to cry.

His mother tried to indicate the path he should take. She told him not to worry, or be upset, "On you go, you will be all right."

Seeing the situation a teacher came over, and presently a solution was found: John his younger brother, although not old enough yet for school, was enrolled too.

George and John, as the teacher taught them the basics, sometimes gazed out at the world through one of the large classroom windows. And although the boys did not know it yet, out there in the big wide world motorcars, aeroplanes, telephones, wireless sets, and X-rays had all been invented. Oil, electricity, coal, wood, wind, and water were now all being used by man for his advantage. The bug that had caused malaria had been found. Miracle drugs, gramophone records, and many other wonders were on their way.

All day the teacher taught them facts and figures, but facts and figures, were just facts and figures, and George and John, like all children, as they gazed out of the classroom window thought the world a fantastic place. Somehow they understood that life out there was linked not together by facts and figures, but by something magical in time and space.

At Busby school every year when the class paid tribute to the fallen, Mary Martin cried, for she had lost a relative in the conflict; her innocent tears seemed to carry the past into the future for her classmates.

Strange though this may sound even though the world had advanced in many ways by the time George and John had gone to Busby school, it was not an uncommon sight, around this time, for a teacher to be hauled out of the classroom by the hair. The angry parent, quite annoyed, shouting: "Don't you ever say that to my boy again!..."

2

By 1920 the population had increased quite a bit in the Parish of Cathcart and, two years after the Great War had ended, when all the soldiers had returned to a land fit for heroes, the family were forced to move away from Clarkston Toll. The house at Rowallandale was tied to the cartwright's business and another cartwright was needed. Thankfully a friend, in the local area, alerted them to another abode not too far away.

George's mother said to the boys one day, "We are all moving into a cottage right in the heart of the country."

And on the day they moved, as they packed their things onto a horse and cart outside the block of flats, at Clarkston Toll, life indeed seemed to be directed by a mysterious force that desired movement and change.

The family, after the furniture had been delivered to the new address, climbed the hill from Waterfoot, just off the Eaglesham Road, and soon they reached the appointed spot. The neglected cottage may have been ignored for a while, but to lovers of life and those looking for somewhere to stay it sat on top of the world.

When they came out of the cottage, after looking around inside, they all gazed down at Glasgow, the metropolis, in the valley below, and when they looked up again they noticed the Kilpatrick Hills, the Campsie Fells, and way out in the distance Ben Lomond.

According to Scottish history, Walter Fitz-Alan, the Great Steward of Scotland, had been responsible for setting up this idyllic spot 'Meikle Dripps' situated halfway between Thorntonhall and Waterfoot.

The white stone cottage opposite Meikle Dripps farm certainly needed a lot of work done to it. The Dripps cottage had been empty for a while, and unfortunately someone had left the door open and the cows had wandered in and out of it at their leisure. The cottage may have been in a bit of a mess, but as far as the young lads were concerned it was wonderful. The house on top of the world had all the secrets of the universe around it.

There was a well not all that faraway next to the house that belonged to the Shaws, and opposite the well a quarry. Meikle Dripps farm, grouped in a U shape, lay right behind the cottage. The farm looked out onto an old Norman motte, now a forest of trees. No one knew if the farmer and his family, the Hendersons, recognized their position on top of the world; for they were solitary people and did not say very much to anyone.

Aunty Bell had by this time returned to Langholm. She wanted to see if she could get work in the mills again. However, another sister arrived to lend a hand. Aunt Agnes was a darner and she could make wonderful things with her hands: leather purses, dresses, trousers, skirts, and handbags. Needless to say it took many hours and many days to knock the cottage into shape, for it really was in a bit of a mess.

In the morning when the natural sunlight came streaming into the cottage at Meikle Dripps, it was as if all the light in the world came through this way before it headed down into the valley. At night when it got dark paraffin lamps were lit so that they could see what they were doing. Thankfully every Friday a man came round on his horse and cart and went round all the farms and dispensed paraffin to those who were running short.

After they got things sorted out aunt Agnes went round the farms during the day doing odd jobs, mainly mending and sowing clothes for the farmers and their workers. Soon they learned that a ploughman had at one time been living in the cottage while working for the farmer.

Certainly, the farming outlook had changed. The accent now seemed to be on producing dairy products; apparently the farmer who owned the land did not need so many workers to work on the land. Someone told George's father that the ground in this area was better suited for cattle, rather than crops.

The owner of the farm, Mr Henderson, charged 3/6p a week for the rent of Meikle Dripps cottage; sometimes at Christmas time he would invite George's father over to play his melodeon at their house. His father had no formal training as regards music; however many years ago the organist at Mearns church had learnt him to read music. He had bought some music books. One was titled, Album of Sacred Songs, and it included the classic tune: 'Angels Ever Bright and Fair,' by Handel.

At night in the cottage he also liked to play popular songs, like the one written by Alan Murray. Young George liked this one:

'I'll walk beside you through the world today
While dreams and songs and flowers bless your way.'

One day Johnny bought a dog, an Irish setter, and they called it Daisy. George's father felt that living so far away in the country a dog would give them security, as well as friendship. Without much trouble a kennel was built for Daisy at the front of the cottage beside the henhouse. Johnny loved dogs and he sometimes groomed them for other people.

It was around this time that confusion as regards a Christian name came about: for when someone around the cottage shouted on George's brother: "John!" the father would always turn round, for his name was John too, although most people called him Johnny. Sometimes it was him that they were after, however more often than not it was young John. So to save confusion George's younger brother was renamed Ian.

The walk to Busby school for George and Ian, from Meikle Dripps cottage, was simply out of this world. In all seasons and in all weathers, every morning, the young lads descended down through the fields.

They soon found themselves in a wonderland of trees, then over burns, fences, and styles they went. George and Ian would usually meet their friends the Shaw twins before they got to the River Cart. Archie and Davy were the same age as Ian.

Sometimes some of the boys would guddle for fish at the dam before climbing up into the plantation, and there in an enclosed world of bounteous creation the boys would stop and collect wild flowers, berries, and birds' eggs. Someone would guess the time, and then they would all head towards the school at Busby.

When they found the river again, parallel to the right of way path, George and Ian would chat with their neighbours the Shaw twins. Life for the young lads was simply out of this world. The fields were full of chestnut and lime trees, oaks, and elms. Life was full of everyday miracles like the beautiful blue star flowers the Forget-me-nots, by the laid near the mill at Waterfoot, or the purple dull flowers the Tufted Vetch, all along the road all the way up to the cottage.

The boys soon found out why it is that beauty for country folk is a small road that cuts across the land and ends up at the sky. They got to know the way of the land. They got to know how the trees and the bushes grow, and how they divide fields into sections and make the world an organized place. In this wonderful time nothing really existed apart from the world they were living in; for nothing had to.

The young lads watched everything around them. They observed every morning how the birds danced for pure joy around the farm. How the Cuckoo came every year to the tree opposite the farm. They watched the dogs run up to the farmhouse, at the back of the cottage, and eat potato skins out of the pots at the front door; they called them pot-lickers.

Yes, every day up at Meikle Dripps they knew they were in for a treat in one way or another. They saw the leaves fall in autumn and die in winter. They saw the first shoots of green life in spring, and they observed how everything in this world comes round again and again before it goes wild once more in summer. In fact at the end of June when the summer sun came out it looked as if the Good Lord had just for a laugh dropped snow down from heaven: for the Hawthorn bushes, daisies, and trees, along with all the other white flowers, made everything for miles look beautiful and unreal.

They could feel the summer sun way out there behind the white and grey clouds, before anyone else could. And when they were at school they could sense the long summer holidays before their classmates. The world on all sides of them, and in all seasons, was full of fields, sometimes buttercups and bluebells, sometimes nothing but grass and earth. And the fields, like life itself, changed with the seasons: for the hand of creation came in the wind, the sun, and the rain, and gently kissed everything.

Every year up at Meikle Dripps, no matter what colours came to the fields, the sheep, the cows, and horses were always there. Foxes and badgers cut across the land day and night. Rabbits and hares every day popped their heads up to say hello to them, before disappearing underground again. The birds: Blue Tits, Coal Tits, Great Tits, Wagtails, Herons, Dippers, Swallows, Woodpeckers, Magpies, Robins, Kingfishers, Blackbirds, and Finches all came in and out of their lives at different times of the year. George loved the birds; they were like old and new friends to him.

All year round the lads watched the farmer and his workers work the land. There were certain drawbacks, however, school was not all that great, but it had its moments like when the teacher locked one of the Shaw twins in the headmaster's room. He meant to deal with him later, but he forgot all about him and went home, and poor Archie had to climb down the drainpipe to escape.

The boys got to know all the country characters, like the man the villagers called Corn Crake, who went round the countryside imitating bird sounds, and who made up his own poems.

Every morning George before going into the classroom - along with all the other boys - would go into the shed and swap comics. His favourite comics were the Rover and the Adventure. Inside the playground, whenever they got the chance, the boys would kick a small tanner ball around.

Knowing that they were living on top of the world, and knowing that there was nowhere else like it anywhere in the universe, George and Ian one day invited all their school pals up to the Dripps for a game of football. The game was to take place in the large field in front of their cottage. It was to be a big game, a final of some kind that would live on in the memory till they were old men.

The game took place, however the farmer did not like this. He didn't say anything about it at the time, but he had a word with George's father later on. In a humdrum tone he said to him, "Tell the boys not to do it again - will you."

Every day during the week mum, knowing the time, would look down from the cottage on top of the world towards the dam. She would watch out for the boys coming back from school; sometimes they would have butter biscuits in their hands that they had bought for her at the Co-op near the school. In the winter the lads were told by the teacher they could get away early at 3.30, for it got dark at 4 o'clock. The teacher knew they had to make their way up to the Dripps.

From the cottage at the Dripps every Sunday they would go to Greenbank church. Mum, if it had been raining - which was more often than not - brought out with her from the cottage two small cloths. And when they got to the narrow road behind the cottage she would clean the boys' shoes, and then she would place the cloths under the wild rose bush at the side of the road. After this country observance they would walk all the way down the road, about two miles, to the church. The boys dressed in their kilts, smart as anything.

Sometimes they would stop just before the country road falls down to the main road, and there they would look in at the grand mansion: The Hill of Birches. They knew the owner of the house was a rich man, named Finlayson. They had heard he was a tailor who made clothes for the well-to-do people in the city. When the Finlaysons went to Greenbank Church they went in a big car.

It seemed at the beginning of the new century one rule above all others seemed to govern the rich: stick together. The maids who worked at the Hill of Birches house liked the local lads, and they would sometimes open the windows of the grand house at festive times, and give the boys some coins. Every year at Halloween the boys would go along there first, and then they would go guising up to Thorntonhall, where the toffs lived. The rich people there were reported to have unbelievable things like: gas cookers, vacuum cleaners, washing machines, and telephones. They had heard that some of them even eat imported food.

The most powerful image down in the valley was the church it seemed to direct everything around it. Sometimes the man who preached there on a Sunday would come and visit the folks up on top of the world during the week. When the minister, Mr Cowley, arrived on his bike up at the Dripps, George thought him very strict, and for some reason the word Victorian seemed to attach itself to the preacher man. George and Ian were both sent out in advance to clean and weed the path, by their parents, when they knew the minister was coming.

There were around 600 members of the church at this time, but some people in the country could remember a time before the word of the Lord was enclosed in stone: a time when the word was passed here and there between people and places: "Jesus down at the River Cart, Jesus on the way to Busby, Jesus at the mill at Waterfoot, Jesus on top of the world, Jesus down at the dam..."

One Sunday, as arranged, after church Mr and Mrs Strang visited the Dripps cottage, bringing with them their two daughters Ada and Hariet. They stayed for a while, had something to eat, and chatted about life and the way of the world in the 1920's. Then everyone, as was the custom of the time, all walked back down the winding road again towards the mill at Waterfoot.

Young George that day had for some reason stayed behind, and later on when everyone had gone he noticed Mrs Strang's umbrella lying just inside the cottage door. She had left it behind.

George picked up the long black umbrella, and as his mind raced he wondered where they would be by now, "They will probably be well past Alexander's Mill," he reckoned, then after a pause, he thought to himself, "in fact they may even be as far as Lethan Farm where John Ross works, or they may even be halfway towards their own home by this time, heading up to the King of the Castle Farm at the Mearns."

Before he could think anymore about it he dashed out of the cottage in a mad hurry, jumped across his heavy framed bike, and went after them. Just by the Hill of Birches he stopped pedalling and looked forward to the descent. George thought about the steep hill that lay in front of him, and before gliding right he looked over towards the Mearns to see if he could see his folks. Unfortunately, the umbrella hanging over the handlebars of course with gravity glided left, the opposite way, towards the bike, and into the spokes. Suddenly young George was catapulted off his bike, and he landed on his right knee on the hard gravel road. For a moment he lay there on the ground with his knee ripped open in front of the ruined bike.

Feeling dazed he got up and after a few moments, in some pain, he hobbled down the shortcut way through the meadow towards the new house that the miller had built for the Shaws. Their house was situated directly opposite the mill at Waterfoot.

Once there young George, like an injured soldier, banged on the door and alerted his neighbours the Shaws about his accident. The family was shocked when they saw him standing there. George asked them to look out for his mum and dad on their way back up to the cottage.

The Shaws had not long moved there from Townhead, by Meikle Dripps, but it was quite normal to have close neighbours a mile or so away at this time in life. Archie's grandfather and grandmother though still stayed up at Meikle Dripps, where they kept Pouter pigeons. Not only had George got to know the twins well by this time, he had also got to know the other Shaws: Louis, John, Robert, Agnes, Myra, who were all younger than him.

Normally when he waited for the twins at the cottage he would stand inside the kitchen and for something to do George would pull and push the water pump that brought the water into the house from the stream outside. He didn't feel like doing that at the moment.

In this part of the country it is true to say that life between 1920 and 1927, was the same for everyone, people hardly deliberated about their existence: "Life was for the living," that's what folks said to you anyway. And when you felt down or depressed, they told you just to get on with it, "Nothing else for it."

After their Sunday stroll, George's parents arrived back at Waterfoot and Mrs Shaw called them in. There may have been

35 million phones in the world at this time, but no one had one up at the Dripps; somebody however found someone in the Waterfoot area who had one, and a doctor was called.

Presently, George hobbled all the way back up the country road to the cottage that sat on top of the world, and when they got there the wound was cleaned. Then after what seemed an age a doctor appeared up at the cottage and clips were inserted into the damaged right knee. George was finally put to bed that day with the instruction to keep his leg straight.

Like all young lads he knew that compensation followed misadventure: in this case missing school for a time and breakfast in bed every morning. Life, in fact for the young lad, had a way of always being fair even when things were disagreeable.

George, lying in bed with his sore knee, couldn't help but wonder about life and all its mysteries - it all seemed so strange. However, the young lad, just like every other young lad who has ever crashed to the ground, may have been injured, but a new philosophy formed in his mind and it seemed to pull him through. He reassured himself, "The episode, I guess, ended not too badly after all."

George, as time went on, got to know everyone connected around the local area: the labourers who stayed in the bothies up at Townhead of the Dripps, and Mr Stoat the Station Master up at Thortonhall, and the girl Gilchrist who lived near Wilson's farm. The Wilsons were nice people; they were always generous to the lads at festive times.

When George and Ian played football down at Waterfoot their mother would shout from the cottage, "Cooee!" and her voice would travel all the way down to the edge of the falls, a good distance away, and let the boys know it was getting late and to come up and get their meal.

One day up at the Dripps they heard a plane overhead. Like most people in the country they had never seen a one-engine plane before. For a time this plane circled round and round, high above the cottage, then suddenly it started to head for the ground. It landed over in the direction of Andrew Barnce's farm.

Everyone in the area who had seen the plane headed towards the field where it landed, not far from the Eaglesham Road. When George got there the pilot had gone, but the folks who were gathered around it said that the pilot was all right and he had been taken away by someone.

When George turned twelve, Wullie, an uncle of the Shaw twins, called at the cottage and boldly asked his mother, "Does George want to go to the Boys' Brigade down at the church, tonight?"

George got ready quickly and he thoroughly enjoyed the evening. And it wasn't long till his brother Ian joined him, and being the right age too so did the Shaw twins, Archie and Davie. So every Friday night from then on, no matter the weather, the boys walked the 2 miles down the road to the Boys' Brigade at the church.

More often than not when George and Ian got to the top of the Hill of Birches, they would look out from under the trees and watch an odd car head up towards Eaglesham. Then after they had passed the mill at Waterfoot, George and Ian, would meet Archie and his twin Davy, and they would walk together down the main road by the little collection of houses: Millerston, Housecraig, Newford, towards the church.

In the summer and in the autumn the lads would pass men and women, arm and arm, heading up towards the falls. The love-birds, amongst them, after billowing and cooing would stroll all the way up to the waterfall, stare at the water, then after a time they would make their way back home towards Glasgow. The lads when they came across them would stare at the town folk, and when caught they would nod at them; for they knew they came from a different world. The lads were told by their parents that the town dwellers came out from Glasgow just to see the beauty of the countryside.

It is true to say that the majority of people in Scotland at this time lived in and around the cities, and would travel on public transport. Someone recorded that there were 960,000 cars in Britain in 1926, if true very few of them went up the road to Eaglesham. Recent reports in the press said that trains and automobiles would one day travel at over a hundred miles an hour. This seemed unbelievable to the people who lived in the country.

Every year George would get a B.B. membership card, and although the front cover changed every year the words on the back always remained the same: 'Remember now thy Creator in the days of thy youth. In all thy ways acknowledge Him and he shall direct thy paths'.

The 223 Boys' Brigade had only been going for two years at Greenbank Church when George joined in 1926. The new minister, Mr Cowley, had a famous cousin, Sir Wm.A.Smith; he had in fact founded the Boys' Brigade in 1883. At the Boys' Brigade they met other boys from the local area, and they learned many things. Yes, the lads looked forward to B.B. every Friday night.

On the way back home up to the Dripps cottage, in the late evening, they would always have such good fun. You could hear them for miles around laughing and joking. George, Ian, Archie, and Davy all played the harmonica. They liked this one:

'Who saw the tattie howker goin awa
Who saw the tattie howker sail in doon the Broomielaw...'

Around about this time Johnny got a job driving a milk lorry early in the morning into Glasgow. The lorry left from Jake Steele's, Newford Farm, and if the River Cart was low Johnny could walk straight down from the house on top of the world and be at the farm in no time at all; however if the Cart was high he had to go all the way down to Waterfoot and along the Eaglesham Road to get to the farm.

They say that Robert Burns must have wandered down this sylvan way once:

> 'Where Cart rins rowin to the sea,
> By monie a flow'r and spreading tree...'

Johnny worked for other farms too, and sometimes he would get work from Sany Graham at Clarkston; Sany was a contractor delivering milk into the city. This is how in fact George learnt to drive, for he would go along with his dad early in the morning and get a shot of the vehicle along the quiet country roads.

Aunt Agnes, his favourite aunt, sent him a bible with best wishes for Christmas. Although many occurrences take place in and around Meikle Dripps area at this time the pace of life never seems to change. Then one day something extraordinary happened: music came down the chimney at the Dripps cottage. It really was unbelievable. Johnny had bought a crystal wax set in town and had fitted a copper aerial on top of the roof of the cottage.

So every night thereafter inside the cottage George and Ian, on the two stools by the fireplace, shared the crystal wax set. Once they mastered how to insert the cat's whisker into the crystal the reception from the set was wonderful, and it soon became part of the routine, inside the cottage on top of the world, just to sit down and relax and listen to the radio George listening to one earphone and Ian listening to the other. The light and heat from the coal fire and oil lamps made everything cosy and warm inside the cottage. Yes, life was wonderful and simple. These were happy days indeed.

3

In 1927 a house became available down at Millerston, just by Waterfoot, on the road to Glasgow. George had passed the small group of houses, situated on the right-hand side of the road, many times before; but he never thought he would one day live there. Someone had told his mother that the houses there were unbelievable: for every house had electricity and there was a toilet on the landing. Even though everyone loved the house on top of the world they were soon on the move again.

Their neighbours at Millerston were friendly people: the Denholms, the McKechnies, the Brittons, the Dochertys, the Herds, the Ross family, Mrs Bryce, Mrs MacColl, and Mr Kirsop the local policeman.

When George was in the city centre of Glasgow with his mother he sometimes saw the red face of Mr McMenemy, the man who lived at the first single end at Millerston. He stood outside the amusement arcade at the Trongate. George thought it funny when some of the rough Glasgow boys shouted at his neighbour, "Hey Mr Panoptican!" but he wasn't sure what they said after that.

Not long after they had settled in at Millerston, Mrs Bryce, when hearing that George's mother was going to see the movie 'The Jazz Singer' gave her some good advice, "Oh, take a towel, dear, it's a weepy!"

27

During the wintertime, a year or two later, a man from the Sunday Post newspaper turned up at the falls and took a picture of George, Jock Shaw, William Alexander, the miller's son, and others, sledging down towards the Mill at Waterfoot. The picture appeared on the front page of the paper, 17 November 1929, with the caption: 'The youngsters had a glorious time sledging yesterday. This picture, taken at Eaglesham, is typical of many throughout the country.'

When the time came George left the only school he had ever known at Busby. He managed to secure a job in the mailroom of the Daily Express newspaper office, in the city centre of Glasgow.

George enjoyed the experience of travelling with people into town every day. And soon without thinking about it too much, like most young people off to work for the first time, he fitted into the daily stream going to and from the city. Life in the city, as in the country, he noticed had a way of being unpredictable. In fact one time he won the Express office sweep, 16 March 1932, and another time he found a purse, 26 Sunday, June 1932, containing 7/3- on the Floors Road, Waterfoot. He kept the money he won, but gave away the money he found to a policeman.

As time went by George followed life's course through the highs and lows, ups and downs, and he tried his best wherever he could to empathize with people involved in the battle of life; Joshua 1,6: 'Be strong and of good courage,' was the motto for 1932 in his B.B. diary. That year he noted down the tragic event that shocked everyone at Millerston: *James Denholm was killed by a car.*

It is true to say that by this time the film industry really hadn't been going for all that long. The history of film in Scotland went something like this: in May 1896, a Glasgow entrepreneur tried out something new called cinematographe inside a store in the middle of town. It was recorded in the press that some

28

people liked it, and some thought it queer. The man obviously wondered if it would catch on. However, by 1910 the first purpose built cinema had opened in the city centre of Glasgow. George's father didn't fancy the movies much, but George, like most young men in the 1930's, went along to the flicks whenever he could. The Picture Halls on the southside of Glasgow were really something special.

George went to the Toledo at Muirend, the Rialto, and the Kingsway at Cathcart, the Crosshill at Govanhill, and the Florida at King's Park. In 1932 he saw: 'Skyline; Palmy Days; Skippy; Mr Bill; Shark; The Conqueror; Brother Alfred; Scarface; The Silent Voice; Animal Dinner; The Crowd Roars; When A Fellow Needs A Friend; The Impatient Maiden.'

Sometimes he would go into the city to the Theatre Royal and see a play. That year he saw, 'Dick Whittington, and Connection with the Yo.Yo.'

His great passion though was football and he played nearly every Saturday for the B.B. On Sunday of course he went to church and sat on pew 56 with the family. In July that year the B.B went to Gullane camp and they all had a fabulous time.

Halfway through 1932 George received an increase to his pay, at the Daily Express office. He noted this down in his diary. 1 July 1932: *I got 4- of an increase in my pay. It is now: £1-12.0.*

George as he got older liked listening into heavyweight championship boxing fights on the radio, but most of all he enjoyed listening to the music. He liked all kinds of music, and on Thursday, 1 September 1932, he went along for the first time to music lessons down at a woman's house in Stamperland.

One night at Millerston, around this time, he switched on his new electric radio and found a familiar station. Then after the programme had finished some original sounds came booming out of it: "That's the end of the programme from the studio tonight, dance music comes from the Mayfair Hotel and will be played by Harry Roy and his band..."

It was absolutely sensational stuff: 'Bugle Call Rag; I Can't Give You Anything But Love; Sentimental Gentleman from Georgia; Sarawaki; Heatwave; Hurricane Harry; It's The Animal In Me;' and on and on it went till midnight.

Apparently, the musical genius in charge of the band came from a box making family down south. He had not all that long ago organized a dance combination known as the Darnswells, along with his brother Sidney. The band had played at the Fitzroy Galleries, London; after this Harry set up another band: The Crichton Lyricals, and toured places like Hammersmith Palais, Cafe de Paris, Oddenino's, Rector's Club, and the Cavour Restaurant. The band then toured South Africa and later Australia, and Germany. Harry after coming back went solo and had led a band at Leicester Square Theatre. His big break came when he played for the first time at the Mayfair Hotel in London.

George wrote to London and joined the fan club and followed all the reports in all the magazines. He received a photo of Harry and his dance orchestra in the post, and some more information, about what the band were up to. It was reported that Harry and his brother, Sidney, organized the band. Harry played the clarinet and composed some of the songs.

The sugar-coated jazz music certainly gave the world a wonderful new rhythm. The music seemed to make fun of life, as it moved up and down the scale. The new jazz appeared to balance the sexes and bridge the gap. What else in life could a young man want - except this wonderful new jazz music? The boisterous band made everything in life worth living for again - thanks to Mr Hocha ma cha-cha. It was absolutely fantastic how the tunes just kept on coming, and how way out there in the towns and country places all over Britain, thousands of other people were listening to the new jazz music too.

It seemed that everything in life, for the new generation, had been made original again; bright lights were going on all over a dark world. This new swing ragtime jazz music would surely change the world - nothing would ever be the same again. The new generation couldn't give you anything but love. They just wanted to be happy - even when they were sad. The swinging jazz on the radio was terrific. No wonder all the young people all over Briton every night were faithfully tuning into it, Wah-De-Dah. And every night the little jack in the box on the radio an hour before midnight would shout to them, "Are you listening?" He had even recorded a song so that his followers could sing it to their mothers: 'Heart of Gold'. So when his folks bought one of those wonderful new gramophone record player's, for the house at Millerston, George rushed out and bought some Harry Roy records and played them whenever he could, nonstop, back to front, start to finish.

Unfortunately, not everyone liked the new jazz music of the early thirties: 'entartete Musik,' they called it. It seemed Fascism was all the rage abroad. Adolf Hitler and Benito Mussolini were the leaders of this new political craze. Fascism had people soon modelling themselves on themselves: for they maintained that if there was no God, then strength and goodness came from the individual: the hero. The Fascists had their own brand of composers and artists, and some folks in Britain were influenced by them.

The Ducu and the man with the funny moustache by 1933 were both well established in their kingdoms. The First World War still troubled the Germans; in fact it troubled anyone who thought about it, for millions had been killed and slaughtered, "And for what?" people asked.

The other great threat, Communism, on the other hand had come out of a revolution: a class struggle against a corrupt state. The Russian people had kicked out their old masters in 1917. However, after the tsar abdicated a new government was formed, but the trouble continued. Then after the October

31

revolution took place a Soviet state came into being and a new political system was set up. The leaders of this movement naturally wanted to export their ideas all around the world. The majority of countries in the West, if not all, for one reason or another, saw communism as an evil. If fascism had, so to speak, put the individual at the centre of things then communism tried to do the same thing with the state. The two regimes were godless and undemocratic.

The young of 1933 knew the world to be an evil place, full of corruption, fear and anxiety, but the new swing pop jazz generation did not worry about it too much. "Life is for the living and life is only worth living if you can make it new, bright, beautiful, and gay," they said.

When the evil world lay over the young they would chase it away by turning an old word into a new word, and suddenly life was wonderful again. That's right life is only worth living if you can love, and show love. The message was in the music and the music was played in swing time. "The world will always be unhappy - what has that got to do with the new swing jazz generation? If you feel down, be happy and down - that's what the new generation say. A world depression may be underway, but there's no need to worry about wars, work, or no work - just dance your life away and be happy and gay."

When the big bands came to town, mainly to the Empire Theatre, George and his friends from the country got all dressed up, and went into Glasgow to see them. And there in the dance halls of Glasgow they had the time of their lives. The live jazz music filled them up with all the illusions present in life.

George in the spirit of the time wanted to join a band - and so he did. On 7 September 1933, after leaving the Boys' Brigade he joined the Old Boys' Association at Cathcart, and there he played the cornet in the band. The band did not play any Harry Roy tunes, but that was all right. When they toured around different places in Scotland they played mainly old Scottish traditional tunes and sometimes songs from shows like The Pirates Of Penzance, etc.

George learned a lot about music during this time, especially the way a band was laid out. And like all music-lovers around the world, he understood the principle that if you follow the melody of a song and let yourself go it can really set you free.

George loved walking down the road in the morning from Millerston to the bus stop, whistling Harry Roy tunes. The sky blue sky, here and there, in between the powder puff clouds seemed to form visions from another world around him. And as he glanced at the country fields, on both sides of him, he felt that they understood everything that came from above. The countryside had nature, and nature had knowledge. Sometimes life just came at him in colours and reflected all the crazy moods inside him.

George, as he passed the fields he knew so well sometimes looked up at the Dripps Cottage, still sitting there on top of the world, and he would smile to himself. The hedges and fields that went all the way up to the cottage had a soothing effect upon his soul. It was as if he could interpret life just by looking at them. He knew the country hills and fields had been there before him, and would always be there throughout his life.

As a young man he understood life in a spiritual way: something hidden never to be revealed. The pace of life and the movement of this world came to him through nature, and that nature he felt sprang from the fields and farms around Meikle Dripps.

George felt to understand life in an ordinary everyday sense you had to watch a swallow fly round a barn. You had to follow a horse that had just bolted, and watch it settle in the middle of a field. You had to watch a man from the city stare at a cow over a fence, and laugh at how the silly thing stared back at him. You had to understand the bark of a dog as it runs towards you along a country road. You had to understand why it is that country roads carry young and old, strangers and demons, up over hills, to their destination. You had to understand why rich people - like those who live up at Thorntonhall - hide from the world behind fences and walls. And you had to understand why death comes in the night and in the day, to rich and poor alike, and how it wipes away all material substance and leaves only spoken words here and there, by and by, for strangers to hear, and others to fear. Yes, life could only be understood when you looked at the country fields between Eaglesham and Busby. George loved the country, and the country boy inside him embraced it with all his heart.

Early photograph of Johnny and his mother at the Mearns.

George gets his picture taken by the local artist,
Tom Lindsay.

George and John up the Mearns Road, 1917/18.

The boys in costume pose,
(right) outside the Hill of Birches.

Deck chairs out on top of the world.

George and Ian with Ada and Harriet Strang.

Outside the cottage with mum and dad.

day Post

Morning Special

BLISHED IN GLASGOW EVERY SUNDAY MORNING.

SUNDAY, NOVEMBER 17, 1929.　　　PRICE TWOPENCE.

,000 PEOPLE TERRORISED

MS

lice :

e.

eat of the
ople.

hadowing
orted that
he is now
Ripper."

ers intima-
milar note-
is either a

murderer,

CKEN.

he frenzy of
iscovery, last
body of five-
nn.
ng of terror
y be gained
past twenty-
wenty people
errogated by
ased immedi-

ustody on the
d boy.

The youngsters had a glorious time sledging yesterday. This picture, taken at Eaglesham, is typical of many throughout the country.

APPEAL FOR SCOTS FISHERMEN	ABERDEEN DOCTOR'S LETTER FROM GAOL.	R101 JOY FLIGHT CANCELLED.
BY SECRETARY OF STATE FOR SCOTLAND.	**GUARDS WHO WATCHED HIM DAY AND NIGHT.**	**LADY M.P.'S CAUSTIC COMMENT.**
Glasgow, Saturday Night. The following appeal on behalf of the Scottish fishermen who suffered such heavy losses in the great gale has been made by Mr Wm. Adamson, Secretary of State for Scotland, to the Lord Provosts of the cities of Glasgow, Edinburgh,	In a letter from Maidstone Gaol, where he has served exact, one year of a life sentence, Dr Benjamin Knowles, the Aberdeen doctor, tells of his trying time after he was arrested, charged with the murder of his wife, formerly Madge Clifton, the actress. "From the time of my arrest"	Because of the weather conditions the projected flight yesterday of R 101 with a complement of about a hundred M.P.s and Peers was cancelled. It is intended, if possible, to make the trip next Saturday, although this will involve some rearrangement, as a number

Sunday Post front page, 17 November 1929.

1st Coy O.B.A Band, first photo 1934.

223 B.B. July 1932.

4

Every year at the end of July at the Glasgow Fair the family would go down to Langholm for the Common Riding. George, Mum, and Ian would all stay for a fortnight, but Dad would usually join then on the second week, for he was always busy working in one of his many jobs.

Johnny, George's dad, loved to sing at the Summer Fair Night. He would normally sing a Burns' song, or some other traditional number from the time of his youth.

When Johnny sang his father-in-law at Langholm felt proud of him. At night he would say to everyone when they came back into the house at West Street: "I, Johnny sang well tonight."

At Langholm the Common Riding, a festival of horse racing and games, starts very early in the morning. The flute band perambulates into town at 5 am playing songs to waken everyone up. Then the Hound Trail begins at 6 30; for a scented cloth of paraffin mixed with aniseed has been dragged around the hills and the dogs follow the scent. Many folk follow the trail and betting is involved. The ceremony at 8 30, is an Assembly of horsemen and the presentation of the town's standard takes place. The provost brings out the standard and the cornet takes it from him. The First Fair Crying is just after this and then the Cornet leads his supporters up the hill towards the monument and the Castle Craigs. The children assemble carrying heather Besoms. About an hour or two later a man stands on horseback in the main square and proclaims the common rights of the people. He declares: "There is a muckle Fair to be hadden in the Muckle toun of Langholm..." Then not long after this the cornet's chase begins. The Common Riding is a wonderful festival that celebrates the right of man to have a share in the land.

George had in fact been named after George Armstrong at Langholm, his mother's father. Grandpa at Langholm, a gas stoker by trade, always maintained that he was related to the famous Border Reiver, Johnnie Armstrong.

So every year, early in the morning at the end of July, they would all set out from the countryside on the southside of Glasgow with their cases. The family would go down the country road, and from there they would travel into Glasgow city centre by bus.

Sometimes they would go to Langholm by Queen Street and then to Edinburgh, via Riddings Junction. Their favourite route, however, was from Central Station to Carlisle, then a nice run up to Langholm. The local train, blowing steam, from Carlisle to Langholm ran on a single track by all the little villages through the unmistakable countryside of the borders. Mum in fact knew the train driver from school, a man called Jordy Jeffrey.

The scenery was wonderful: secret woods and small roads would suddenly appear all running along with the train before disappearing round bends, then the woods and the roads would appear again this time with villages and farmhouses round them.

And as they approached the mills at Langholm grandpa would appear standing outside the first mill, Neils's Mill, and he would wave to them. He knew the time of the train that they would be on. Then once he had seen them he would go back inside the grey sandstone building, where they made cloth for all over the world, and go back to work again.

A brass band played the visitors off the last train at Langholm station, and the holidaymakers, travellers, bookies, and hounds, who were part of the festival in the morning, all marched behind them. And just round the corner Granny would be waiting for them at the Gas Entry, a small lane that led to the gas works near the station, where Grandpa used to work; and from there they would travel a short distance to the house at 3 West Street. When they got there Uncle Jimmy would appear at the top of the stairs. He would laugh and shout, "Here come the Glasgow Keelies!" before coming down the stairs to greet them.

And during the holiday they would see aunty Jeanie, aunty Bell, uncle Tom (who carried the Barley Banner), aunty Lizzy from Selkirk, and aunty Maggie, and many other nephews, cousins, and friends. They were great days indeed at Langholm.

George and Ian, being country boys, would roam about all over the town, up to Whita Hill and look at the monument dedicated to Sir John Malcolm, then back down again. Naturally, the boys as they went about the town would think about a time gone by: a time before motorcars and trains, when the roofs had not yet been slated; and their young minds marvelled about what it must have been like when the stagecoach came through here twice a day. Great Grandpa they were told used to drive the stagecoach from Hawick to Langholm, and they were told that he used to carry a blunderbuss gun. They tried to read the past in people's faces, and sometimes they would catch a glimpse of a previous time in this or that face as it passed them by on the street. The invisible thread that carries the past into the present always made them smile.

When the boys got to Skippers Bridge, they would drink icy cold water from the mountainside, from a metal cup that had a chain on it. Then they would watch a car, or two, head up the road to Newcastleton, towards Maggie's farm, where she lived with her husband Sandy Anderson, the shepherd.

In 1933 a great event for them took place at Langholm: Uncle Jimmy was elected to be cornet. Uncle Jimmy would now fall into legend: the first Armstrong to be crowned cornet. "The greatest day of a man's life!" so they say in this part of the world.

Grandpa at Langholm told the boys that they were related to the border Reiver Johnny Armstrong, and like magic he would, just by a few words, transport them back to another world. He spoke about the debatable land; how the Border Reiverers roamed, stole cattle, killed, plundered, kidnapped and conquered. He told them stories about the Armstrongs, who came from Liddesdale, valley of the song, and how they were the most lawless of them all. He explained the past to them, how they lived in huts, how they worked as millers and blacksmiths, and how they roamed about here and there: "On the border was the Armstrongs, able men, somewhat unruly and very ill to tame..."

George and Ian were enthralled, and as the two young lads listened they wondered about their blood relations, the desolate marshes where Reivers went to hide, and the towns and market places of the surrounding area. The names of the places seemed so strange: Tarras Moss, Chipchase, Buccleuch, Annadale, and so did the characters, Black Jock, Tower of Sark, Kinmount Wullie. And the expressions they used at that time inside the debatable land: 'ye auld tyme, white mail, hot trod, truce signs, deep pools and murder holes, ye ken'.

The lads discovered how men drank from the lakes and streams, how free booters could make money on the hoof. One time a father once went on a raid and found that it was his son's house that they were planning to raid. The man sat that one out, but he joined in on the next one. The lads learned how the folks would place white cloths on hedges and bushes, here and there, around the countryside, and beacons on all sides, so as to warn their neighbours a raid was going on.

One story about an Armstrong was very interesting indeed. He was returning from London when he came across some of Cromwell's men near the bridge over the River Eden, not far from Carlisle. The man heard their hoofs and reckoned an ambush was about to take place, and when they charged him from both sides he drove his horse over the bridge and into the water. A roundhead gave chase, but retreated at the sight of a steel pistol; he obviously forgot the powder was wet.

Another tradition from the debatable lands fascinated the lads, Hand-fasting: how men and women would go down to where the black and white Esk rivers meet and join hands and an engagement was made, whereby in a year's time they would come back again and see how things stood between them.

However, after all that the dominant character from the past, Johnnie Armstrong, seemed more real than time itself. He seemed at times too powerful even for a king to handle.

One day, when the warden Cary was out looking for the Armstrongs, the people of Liddlesdale slipped over the border and plundered the warden's land. On the way back they sent him one of his own cattle just in case he went hungry.

The Armstrong clan for years fought the warden and his men inside the debatable land, and yet strange as it sounds on a Saturday at Carlisle market they would all walk by him and smile at him.

The king despaired saying, "Why is this so; the Armstrongs have blackmailed and killed, and have been banned from the market place."

However, like all adventures, the story had to come to an end, and Johnnie Armstrong was summoned to meet the new king. So one day dressed in his fine clothes he, along with 30 others, presented himself to the monarch and a thousand of his men.

King James V, seeing Johnnie in all his splendour, asked: "What wants that knave that a king should have?" and turned away and gave the order for execution: "Kill them all!"

One of Johnnie's followers broke through the ranks and carried the news to Gilnockie Tower. That day they say Johnnie Armstrong's wife heard the tragic news with his son by her knee.

So Johnnie and his followers were hanged upon growing trees at Carlenrig Chapel, not far from Langholm, and to this day the people of the borders say that because of the injustice a king brought to bear on a well-known man, the trees around that part of the country have withered away.

"I that is the story of Johnnie Armstrong," Grandpa would sigh and say.

'Sum speikis of lords, sum speikis of lairds,
And sick lyke men of hie degrie;
Of a Gentleman I sing a sang,
Sum tyme called the laird of Gilnockie.'

5

It took the good part of a day to get from Langholm to Millerston. However, they knew they were back from their holidays when the bus entered the familiar surroundings of Clarkston. After Clarkston it was mostly fields all the way up to Eaglesham. It didn't take the bus too long to climb from the toll up towards the country. Thankfully the bus stop where they got off, on the left-hand side of the road, was not all that far from where they stayed at Millerston.

Now on this same road every day of the week, except Sunday, a man would stop his sour-milk cairt right outside the small group of houses at Millerston. The man after getting down from his cairt would stand at the back of it, not all that faraway from the Clydesdale horse. On the barrel at the back of the cairt was a tap and from that tap he would fill jugs, that people brought to him, up with sour-milk.

The man came from one of the farms beyond Eaglesham - either the Allan of the Inches or Picken of Park Farm - and in the morning he would travel down to Clarkston, and then on to Cathcart.

In the early evening as the sun was going down near to the land opposite Millerston, the sour milk cairt could always be seen heading back up the road again towards Eaglesham. The man slumped up against the barrel fast asleep with his bunnett down over his eyes. It was just as well the old farm horse knew

41

the way home. Someone in the local area who witnessed this scene made up a song about it (Andrew Dunbar).

'I am a country chappie, I'm serving at Polnoon,
A fairm near Eaglesham, that fine auld-fashioned toon,
Whar wi' the milk each mornin' a little after three
We tak' the road right merrily, my old black horse and Me.
The ither mornin' early, as the Borlins I did pass,
I chanced to forgather wi' a bonnie kintra lass.
Says I, my winsome lassie, if ye be gaun that airt,
I'll drive ye into Glesca on my sour-milk cairt.
Then linkin' on thegither, we wad wander to Milkha'
To pu' the sweet wild roses roon Polnoon auld castle wa';
Gaun hameward in the gloamin' I wad press her to my
heart, And remind o' her promise in the sour-milk cairt.'

Sometimes George would keep a diary and, like everybody else, at the end of the year he would look back and reflect upon the events. Diary of 1934:

JANUARY

MON. 1, Went to Hampden with father, Queens 4 v Third Lanark 2. Pictures at night, Successful Calamity. SUN. 7, Working squaring the ledger; church in the morning. WED. 10, Band practice in the Labour Hall. SAT. 13, Went to the Toledo, Storm at Daybreak. SUN. 14, Old Boys' Church Parade to Kings Park. The band's first time out. It was pouring with rain. THUR. 18, Piano lessons at Stamperland with Miss Gray. FRI. 19, Band practice; got measured for a suit by Mr Strang. SAT. 20, Went to Hampden with Wullie Lang and Ian Howden, Queens Park 1 v Forfar 0. SUN. 21, Went to the office a couple of hours to finish the statement. WED. 31, Mr Strang brought down my new suit.

FEBRUARY

FRI. 2, Got 10- of a rise, my wage is now £2-10-6. SAT. 3, Played football, Daily Express 1 v Larkfield Am 7. WED. 7, Old Boys' Band Practice. SAT. 10, Was reserve for the Express Team. MON. 12, Union meeting, then to the Pavilion with A Stronack and Dave Willis to see Aladdin. Then went for Billiards. FRI. 15, Piano lessons. SAT. 17, Played football for Express 0 v Stewarts & Loyds 1. SUN. 25, Old Boys' Parade to Cathedral, Band playing. TUES. 27, Went with Douglas Anderson to Thomson's Dancing Academy to learn, 10/6 for 15 lessons. WED. 28, Band practise in Battlefield Hall.

MARCH:

THUR. 1, Piano lessons. FRI. 2, Band practise. SAT. 3, Played for Express 2 v Yoker Team. 3. TUES. 6, Dancing lessons at Thomson's Cumberland Street. WED.7, Piano lessons, Band Practise. SUN. 11, Church Parade of the Old Boys' Association to Church in Lockleaven Road. MON. 12, Started on Rail Dept. SAT. 17, Played for the Daily Express 1 v McFarlane Lang 4. FRI. 23, Tommy Waterston was married. SUN. 25, Working till 9pm. WED. 28, My last piano lesson with Miss Gray. Then Band practise. FRI. 30, Working late till 11 o'clock.

APRIL

TUES. 3, Dancing lessons. FRI. 6, Old Boys' Association dress rehearsal in the Couper Institute. Day off for working on Sunday. SUN. 8, Church parade with band the 2nd Old Boys' Association to Hutchestown Church, then went to my work. MON. 9, Union Meeting, then played David Brown at billiards. SAT. 14, Went to the Kingsway with Willie Lang to see Moonlight Melody. MON. 16, Working late all month. THUR. 26, Archie Shaw broke his ankle. FRI. 27, Old Boys' night out to the Florida.

MAY

SAT. 5, Went to Langholm by the 1.30. MON. 7, Came back from Langholm. THUR. 10, Went down to see Captain about arrangements for the B.B. Display. SUN. 13, Went to the dedication of the B.B. colours, straight from work; had to take collection. THUR. 17, Half-Day off. MON. 21, Played football down at Giffnock. FRI. 25, Half-Day off, Band practice. SUN. 27, Working, church in the morning. WED. 30, Working till 10pm.

JUNE

FRI. 1, Half-Day off; Old Boys' Band practise. WED. 3, Working till 9pm all week. FRI. 8, Band practise. TUES. 12, Played for Clarkston team 1 v Georgestown Select 1, I was centre half. FRI. 15, Day off; O.B.A band practise. SAT. 16, Went down to St. Aidan's Scout sports with O.B.A. FRI. 22, The Farmers flitted; band practice. WED. 27, Went to Cathkin Park with Archie Shaw to see Benny Lynch fight J Campbell. FRI. 29, Working till 11pm, got last bus. SAT.30, Working till 4pm.

JULY

SUN. 1, Working all week, no day off. FRI. 6, Working till 12 pm, got a bus to Giffnock then walked the rest. SUN. 8, Went to Busby Baths with James and John Docherty then went to work at 2pm. MON. 9, Working till 9.30pm, off from 12.30 till 4pm for dinner. THUR. 12, Day off went to the dam for a dook in the afternoon. SAT. Not working, went to the hay, then went to the Linn Park with W Bryce. TUES. 17, Started in the Contributions Department. SUN. 22, Walked over to the Mearns with dad to see granny. WED. 25, Went a cruise at night fare 3/3. FRI. 27, Went down to help father at Lawrence's garden. SUN. 29, Walk with Arthur Ross away round by Steels' and Thono farms.

AUGUST

WED. 1, Went to the Toledo Pictures with Arthur Ross, W Brownlee. THUR. 2, Working late till 9pm. SAT. 4, Rangers sports with Joe Britton, W Bryce and Ian. SUN. 5, Went to Busby Baths in the morning. SUN. 19, Archie Shaw and I went a walk and took photographs. SAT. 25, Left for Langholm with the 2 o'clock. MON. 27, Went up to Maggie's farm with cousin Walter on the bicycles. FRI. 31, Went to the pictures.

SEPTEMBER

SAT. 1, Went to Carlisle with Aunty Jeanie to meet father. SUN. 2, Went to see the big stone up at Wauhope with Walter. Mon. 3, Left Langholm for Glasgow.

George, after his holiday, should have started back to work on the Monday in the second week of September 1934, at the Daily Express Office, but on the Friday of that week he fell ill. The Doctor was called and understanding the seriousness of the situation, he paid three visits thereafter.

The simple note in the diary, 7 September 1934, did not in anyway indicate how grave the situation was: *Took ill. Doctor paid three visits.*

Saturday, 8 September 1934: *Doctor paid 2 visits.*

Everyone was clearly worried; for George kept bringing up blood. After some consultation Ian, his younger brother, was sent by the doctor down to Tony Equi's Cafe at Busby for ice. When Ian came back, the doctor told George to suck the ice. He was told that he could not eat a thing until the blood stopped.

Thankfully the vomiting of blood ceased, but George spent the whole month of September in bed. The doctor called every Thursday thereafter.

The next month, October, he was still not able to get up on his feet and, Hamilton Wright, the dentist from Cathcart, called at the house and took two teeth out. There was no way, George, in his condition could have managed to go down to the surgery.

Unfortunately, at the end of the month a Registered Letter came through the letter box at Millerston from his employer, D Alexander, Chief Accountant, at the Daily Express, dated 30 October 1934:

'Dear George, I trust that you are still making progress towards recovery, and soon will be quite fit again for the battle of life. No doubt you will appreciate that with the mechanization of the Counting House there are several people being displaced, and I am sorry to say that you are one of the number.'

George had worked there for over five years, and now he was being paid off. It had been a good wage too, and he would miss all the people who worked there. He felt that it would not be the same going to the Nile Billardroom if he had not been to a Union meeting beforehand; however that was the least of his worries at the moment. The staff sent him a 'get well' card and wished him all the best:

'Dear George, The staff have sent under separate cover some books, which I trust will enable you to enjoy your convalescence. They also wish me to convey their best wishes for a speedy and complete recovery, also for a Merry Christmas and Happy New Year when it comes.' Peter Clark. PS: Hope to get along to see you shortly.

Thankfully the terrible month of October slowly passed away and, at the beginning of November 1934, George was able to see some visitors. Capt Coupar, the nice man at the head of the Old Boys' Association, came to see him and tried to help him.

He was allowed out for the first time for one hour on Friday, 2 November 1934. Mr Cowley, the minister, and John Paterson came to see him the following week.

On 9 December 1934, the following month, George celebrated his 20th birthday. He got a set of military brushes from his parents. John Ross, from Millerston, and Archie and his twin Davie Shaw, called in to see him just before Christmas. Their visit cheered him up no end.

On Christmas Eve he went to Greenbank Church, and on Christmas Day John Paterson and Bert Nicol came out to see him, and took him for a run in the car.

Mr Strang, the tailor, on the last day of the year brought down a new coat for him to wear. It had been a funny old year looking back on it, the ups and downs, the battle of life right enough. The world he had known at the start of the year had somehow disappeared, and now he was not sure of the future anymore. George knew that he had to build up his strength and get back into the swing of things - although he knew there would be no football for a time.

The year 1934 ended on a strange note, the MP Winston Churchill warned the people of Britain about German air strength, but very few people took any notice, most folk felt that it wouldn't come to anything.

6

One year went by and then another new one came in, but still no one seemed to have the answers to the following questions: "Why has the world fallen into decline? Why does bust always follow boom? Why are there so many people out of work?"

Some optimists, by the mid-thirties, thought the worst had past, others reckoned it had still to come. Meanwhile, the bankers tried to explain to the politicians where all the benefits had gone to from the last decade. The politicians naturally blamed each other. Some experts in the press offered excuses. The ordinary people, who had probably a better reading of the situation, however, just got on with things as best they could.

George, when talking to friends, would try to make light of the situation, "It's a funny thing life," he would say to them, "but don't let it get you down."

With pride and resilience he visited the Labour Exchange every Friday morning. George understood that he had a good mum and dad, but he also knew that he had to find a way of generating a spare bit of cash. The young lad wherever he could, in and around the local area, tried to make a bob or two here and there; for he knew there were many things to do in life at the age of 22. Things may have been tight but, like all young men, George loved to go to the dancing and to the pictures. He also tried, whenever he could, to put some money aside so that when the big bands came to town he could go along with his friends and see them.

Grandmother, as she had done many times before on the first day of the year, came down from the Mearns to Millerston to wish everyone a happy new year. It wasn't a great day to first-foot people though: for the weather was poor and it rained all day.

In the evening, as was customary at this time of the year, George went out to the dancing. He had arranged something with Peter Stewart last week. George's friend lived at the Sheddens just down the road from Millerston. Peter's mother had a dairy there not far from the Buckshead pub. That night on the first day of the year, 1936, they went to a Carnival Night at the Diamond Dancing Academy down near the Gorbals.

There must have been about 70 places where you could go dancing at this time in Glasgow; everyone it seemed just loved to dance. Every night in Glasgow young men and young women would go Jigging, and enjoy themselves. It was wonderful entertainment.

In the 1920's the Dancing Academy had been very strict; in fact they say if you were not dancing correctly at that time a man came up to you and tapped you on the shoulder with a stick. Ten years later it may not have been so strict, but good dancers were still in demand in dance halls in Glasgow. George loved to dance, and he went to the Dancing Academy whenever he could.

Every Friday evening he went to the O.B.A: the Old Boys' Association. The Company at Cathcart, a Christian movement, had been formed, on the 16 September 1927, for essentially ex-members of the Boys' Brigade. Twenty-seven lads had turned up that night at Mount Florida school. When George joined the O.B.A, the Association had 13 companies, with one in Wick, and one in Falkirk.

The Toledo Picture Hall at Muirend was another outlet in life for George. The Toledo was situated on the left-hand side of the road halfway between Millerston and Glasgow. The Eaglesham bus dropped the filmgoers, from the southside, right outside the door of the Toledo.

The Toledo, built by William Beresford, looked like it had been transported over to Glasgow from some SpanishAmerican town. And the strange building sometimes appeared to the eye as if it could fly away any minute back to Spain. The picture hall, however, thanks to the thousands of people going in and out of it, had remained stationary since it had touched down on 2 October 1934. All the young filmgoers from the south side hoped that it would stay open indefinitely; for they loved going to the Toledo at least once or twice a week.

It was reported in the press that TV sets were now on sale. Another report followed saying that about 280 of them had been sold - but who in their right mind wanted to stay in when you could go out to the flicks.

On Thursday, 9 January 1936, George went to see 'George's White's Sandals,' and feeling part of the new jazz age he put on his soft hat for the first time. The film featured the song 'Nasty Man,' sung by Alice Faye. George enjoyed the film though he preferred the Harry Roy version of the song. Yes, picture houses on the southside of the city were great places to go to for entertainment, especially in the winter. And it was true what people said about the medium: "If you let yourself go, moving pictures will really transport you to another world."

That afternoon George got off the bus and stood there in a little queue, then once inside the Toledo picture hall he found a seat, somewhere in the middle of the stalls, and under a dark blue mystical ceiling his country life simply disappeared. Little lights flickered, then the dark curtains, full of strange shadows, matadors and butterflies, slowly opened and away he went...

When he came back to reality George noticed that life, just like the pictures, had surprises around every corner. Some days he would feel fine, then the next he didn't feel too well at all,

"That's life," he would say to himself.

When in conversation about the world George would sometimes use the phrase, "The battle of life," then sigh and say, "that's it." The man who had terminated his contract of employment had used the same phrase.

Unfortunately, the monarch, King George V, at the beginning of the week gave up the battle of life and passed away aged 71, and when George came back from the Rialto picture house that night, after seeing 'False Face,' he noted the event down in his dark blue diary. The picture inside his diary of Windsor Castle, where kings and queens lived and died, seemed to be from another world. Maybe one day he would visit the castle and see it for himself.

Monday, 20 January 1936: *The King died tonight at 11.55 pm.*

Mrs McColl at Millerston, not so well known to the world, took ill at the beginning of the new month and passed away on Saturday, 8 February 1936.

Tuesday, 11 February 1936: *Today was the funeral of Mrs McColl, the cortege left Millerston at 12.20pm for the crematorium at Maryhill.*

Country life went on as usual and, at the end of the month, Mr and Mrs Adair, friends from Rowallandale, and Mr and Mrs Dugan came for tea as usual; and all the recent events, near and far were discussed. Sadly at the end of the month another good neighbour passed away.

Thursday, 20 February 1934: *Mrs Docherty died this morning.*

Sometimes George would wander up to the Mearns to see if his Granny was all right. When he was younger she used to give him half a crown - which was a lot of money for a young lad in these days - out of the kist in her room. Granny Bowman kept by the fireside an old horseshoe. She once told George the horseshoe had come off a horse that had been in the Boar War, and the silly old thing seemed to bring her luck.

Aunty Bell arrived from Langholm, 1 March 1936, for a day

trip. George and his father went to collect her in Mrs Tulloch's taxi car. The big bands arrived in town too that month and George went along to see them: Ivor Morton and Dave Kay at the Empire, 2 March 1936, Billy Cotton and his band, 9 March 1936, and Lita Grey Chaplin, 16 March 1936. At the end of the month aunt Agnes telephoned a neighbour, the Herds, saying that she too was coming up to Glasgow. When she arrived George and aunt Agnes went down to Inchinin to see the Queen Mary leave the fitting out basin for Southampton.

George recorded the trip in his diary: Tuesday, 24 March 1936, *We had an excellent view.*

Meanwhile, in another part of the world the German elections, 29 March 1936, got under way, and the Nazi party won 99% of the vote. Mussolini nationalized the Italian banks. It was also reported on the radio around this time that Austria was just about to bring in conscription.

The Old Boys' Association had a display coming up soon, so every Wednesday in April George pencilled in his diary: *rehearsal at Gary Street.*

On Good Friday John Ross came over and they went for a run in the motorcar up to Walton Farm. George got a shot at driving the car along the quiet country roads. Still very keen on music, he went up to Bradley's, Dundas Street, Glasgow, the following Thursday to inquire about piano tuition; and once there he arranged a few dates for some music lessons.

Saturday, 18 April 1936: *Mother left at 8.50 to spend the weekend in Langholm. Father went to the Cup Final. I went to the Rialto at night with Peter, to see Hands Across The Table.*

The picture the following Monday at the Rialto at Cathcart, that George went to see, seemed to be straight out of life. 27 April 1936: *Went to see the picture Off The Dole.*

However, not to worry the golf season, at the beginning of summer, had benefits for all the local lads in the area. George, on the first Saturday of May 1936, headed up to Bonnyton

Moor Golf Course. The course lay in the direction of Eaglesham, and was run by Jews. On the first day up at the course he caddied for a Mr Pringle and received 2/6. And the following Monday he caddied for a party from Weir Pumps, Cathcart.

A sad event, however, took place in the middle of the month when a young friend was buried.

Monday, 18 May 1936: *I was down at the Funeral of April Dugan at Thonliebank.*

George, with some of the money he had made from caddying, bought a new pair of shoes, but he knew by the end of the week his dole money would stop, and thereafter he would be on a Means Test. The film on at the Kingsway at Cathcart the following Saturday, that he went to see, had a certain ironic ring to it: 'We're in the Money'. Thankfully things picked up at the end of the month and his luck changed.

Thursday, 21 May 1936: *On looking through the paper this morning I came across a horse named Royal Romance, as this is the same name as Harry Roy's picture, I thought I would back it. I put 6p each way on it and it won. I got 1/6 back.*

Wednesday, 27 May 1936: *Went in to the Labour Exchange to get my insurance card stamped, then I proceeded to Dunn & Co shop in Argyle Street to see about a job for Saturday's. I got home at 12.45, and at 1.30 I left for the golf course, but there was nothing doing.*

The month of June kicked off with some of the members of the Old Boys' Association band going up to the Orange Hall in Cathedral Street to play at a meeting.

Monday, 1 June 1936: *I let my cornet fall while waiting for some of the lads at Battlefield, but it didn't affect the tone.*

George took the cornet into town on Wednesday up to Bradley's shop, just to make sure, and he picked it up on Friday after his piano lesson. It cost him 2/6 to sort the bash.

The first Annual display of the Old Boys' Association took

place in Cathkin Park on Saturday 6 June 1936. The guest of honour was Sir Ian Colquhoun.

Report by a local correspondent: 'On the green sward of Cathkin Park and on the slopes of the enclosure opposite the grandstand there was re-enacted on Saturday the stormy story of the Covenanters. The pageant realistically unfolded three of the major episodes in the struggle of that dour band of men who, persistent in their loyalty to the Presbyterian form of worship, carried weapons with them to their field preachings.'

The following week George managed to get a caddie on Tuesday, Wednesday, and Saturday; he also found a shilling on the golf course on Tuesday, making it 3/6 that day.

Sometimes on a good day he could get two caddies at Bonnyton Moor, like on Wednesday, 17 June 1936: *After dinner I went up to the golf course, I had a good day today. I got 2/6 from a Mr Crawford, then at 8 o'clock I caddied for Mr Chalmbers and got 3/- for ten holes, making a grad total of 5/6.*

George started at Dun and Co. Argyle Street, at the end of June 1936, and he got paid 7-6 for the day.

Sunday, 21 June 1936: *Went to the Linn Park with Donald and John Adair, and the boy Scott to hear Foden's Silver Band.*

It was mostly men who golfed up at Bonnyton Moor, however one day George caddied for a woman.

Tuesday, 23 June 1936: *I was up at the course today, I got two rounds, first a man in the afternoon, then a lady at night. 2/6 from each making 5-.*

The Bankers' Tournament took place at Bonnyton Moor on the 24 June 1936, and George caddied for a Mr Louden. He gave him 4/6. If the game went on late up at the course - sometimes well past eleven - he had to cycle home. He went down the Floors Road, then along the dark country lanes and, if the moon was not out and the clouds were drifting here and there hiding the stars, it could be quite dangerous, for he had no light on his bike.

The following week was a busy week for George. He caddied for a professional golfer.

Monday, 6 July 1936: *I went up to the course at 10.am today and I caddied for D Cobb, professional golfer. He was practising for a tournament on Wednesday.*

Tuesday, 7 July 1936: *I caddied for the Dunlop Golf Ball Traveller: he gave me 2/6 and a golf ball. Mark Seymour scored a 65.*

George phoned his old newspaper the Daily Express with the result. In the middle of the week the Glasgow professional golf championship started and George was up at the course early that morning.

Wednesday, 8 July 1936: *I was up at Bonnyton Moor at 9.45. I was caddying for Mr A Ritchie from Greenock. 2 rounds I got 6/-.*

Thursday, 9 July 1936: *After I came home from the Labour Exchange I caddied for a Jew and got 2-6 for 14 holes. It was a light bag too. At night I got out with Myat Harris he gave me 2/6*

Friday, 10 July 1936: *I went up to the golf course at 9.30. There was to be a game on at 10 am, but they didn't play till 12.30. I caddied for Mark Seymour and received 2/- for nine holes.*

Sometimes, after church on a Sunday, George would go down and see the Adairs, now living at Cathcart. And after tea he would go with them to the Rouken Glen Park.

George, at the beginning of the week on his way to work, got his mother and father into town on the bus. It was the Glasgow Fair Saturday, and they were off to Rothsay for their holidays this year. Unfortunately, George had to work on Fair Saturday at Dun and Company, but he went down the coast the next day, along with John Ross, and joined them. And on Tuesday some other folks arrived. His brother Ian, and Willie Young came over from Dunoon, and so did Mr and Mrs Adair. The boarding house was soon packed with holidaymakers. Thankfully most of them left the next day.

Wednesday, 22 July 1936: *Mother and father and I went for a cruise to Lockgilphead from Rothsay tonight it cost 1/9, coming home there was singing and dancing on board.*

Of course it rained nonstop, as it does down the coast during the Glasgow Fair, but it didn't seem to worry anyone. The following week they left Rothsay for home at 10.35.

Saturday, 25 July 1936: *It was wet, and the boat (the Duchess of Fife to Wemyss Bay) was doing a bit of rolling about in the stormy water, then the train for Glasgow.*

Mrs Hunter, from St Aidan's Clarkston, knowing George's father to be a keen dog handler, asked him to keep a dog for her; so a little Scotch Terrier named Gyp for a time roamed around their house.

After the month of July had faded away the harvest got under way and another source of income materialized for George.

Monday, 3 August 1936: *I went up to the hay at Andrew Renfrew's farm today and got 4/-.*

George the next day went up to the golf course and thereafter kept that rota going all week.

The following week a big tournament took place up at Haggscastle Golf course, on the southside of Glasgow, so George went over to see if he could get a caddie, but he was unsuccessful and he returned home.

Later that day Mr and Mrs Connal came up to Millerston; they had heard about a job that might be suitable for George. His mother in the past had worked for them, part time, tending their house. They had obviously heard about George being out of work.

The next day he went for an interview to M. L. Thomson Hatters, Union Street, but it was somebody with experience they were looking for. The man who interviewed him, trying to alleviate the disappointment, asked George why he did not have his hat on; for all the young men were wearing them now. Maybe if he had worn his soft hat he would have got the job - such is life.

After the hay on Saturday at the farm, George was paid 5/6-. Then he went with a friend to the trot at the Eaglesham shows; there he backed 'Mae West' in the final race, but it came in second.

With the summer coming to an end, the football season started again. George played his first game of the new season towards the end of the month.

Saturday, 28 August 1936: *I was playing at Muirend for the Old Boys' Association 5 v 1 Mount Florida.*

George, on the first day of the new month, even though it was raining, headed up to the course. He managed to get a round in, and for his trouble was duly paid 3/- then he hurried back down to Cathcart to play for the Old Boys' Association.

Tuesday, 1 September 1936: *We played a player short the whole game. O.B.A. 1 v 4 Forsth Memorial.*

The pattern of life, as autumn faded into winter, seemed to be set out for the rest of the year: football on a Saturday, piano lessons during the week, and Old Boys' Association every Friday night.

On 15 September he carried a bag around the Bonnyton Moor course for a Frenchman. The Frenchman managed the Grovnor Hotel in town. He gave him 2/6.

George had managed, by the middle of the month, to get quite a few caddies in, and it was just as well for his favourite big band was coming to town.

Wednesday, 16 September 1936: *I went up to the Empire Theatre and booked seats for Harry Roy for next week, I then went to the golf course and got the Frenchman. He picked me out of the crowd of caddies, 2/6.*

Sometimes up at Bonnyton Moor golf course you came across some interesting characters.

Wednesday, 30 September 1936: *I got out in the afternoon, I was caddying for the green-keeper, he was playing some gentleman who had plenty of money; he paid for the caddie fee 3/9 and then he offered us a drink, I took the money 8d, total 4/5.*

Saturday, 3 October 1936: *I was playing at Netherpollock for the O.B.A, 5 v 2 Wells Memorial.*

Tuesday, 6 October 1936: *I was out at Stirling's Potatoes today, and was my back sore, I had to go to bed early at night. I am getting 4/- a day.*

With all this running around it was no wonder George did not feel well again.

Thursday, 8 October 1936: *I fainted this morning when I came in from the lavatory. I was very sick for an hour; however by 10 am I was a bit better and went out potato picking.*

His mother was also not feeling to well and the doctor was called in on the morning.

Friday, 16 October 1936: *I was out at Renfrew's (Barrance Farm) potato picking; at night I was at St Andrew's Hall playing in the church Old Boys' Association.*

Not many golfers went out onto the course when it rained, and of course this reduced George's income. The weather at the end of October was not good; in fact it rained from start to finish.

Monday, 26 October 1936: *Peter and I went to the Toledo to see Strike Me Pink. The programme had to be abandoned owing to the roof being blown off by the hurricane; no one was injured. We got complimentary tickets.*

On the last Saturday of the month, George helped with the jumble sale at the church hall for the Old Boys' Association in Thistle Street, and in the afternoon he played for the team against Crosshill at Queens Park recreation ground; they won 6-2.

Meanwhile, on the world stage Mussolini secured an agreement with the Germans. They would now be called the Axis. Roosevelt was re-elected as US president. Switzerland, France, and Holland all came off the Gold Standard. Germany recognized Franco's Spain.

George, at the beginning of November 1936, went into town to the Daily Herald office; he had heard they were looking for workers. He was told to come back at 2pm, and so that afternoon he joined a class to become a canvasser.

On the first Saturday in November, he went over to the People's office and there he received instruction and a ticket that would take him to Ayr the following Monday. Apparently, they were going to promote the paper down the coast. George then went and played football for the Old Boys' Association 3 v 5 Abbotsford Chalmers.

Monday, 9 November 1936: *I was up at 5am this morning to catch the 7 o'clock train at St Enoch's station for Ayr, to canvass for the 'People'; arrived in Ayr with 3 others at 8.30. We went straight to the supervisor. I got 5 orders all day. We got lodgings for the week for 5/-.*

The next day they were sent to Mayboyle and there they canvassed till 6pm at night, then they got the bus back to Ayr. George managed to secure 8 orders. It was the same on Wednesday, however George only managed to get 1 order this time, and when they came back to Ayr, because of the lack of sales, three of the canvassers were paid off.

Thursday, 12 November 1936: *We got up early at 7am; had to meet the supervisor at 8.30 and hand in our papers and leaflets. We got 31/9 for 4 days work.*

To celebrate George and some of the lads went to the pictures down at Ayr, to see 'Small Town Girl', then they headed back to Glasgow on the 7,05 train.

George, during the last week of November, went back up to Bonnyton Moor golf course and he managed to get out a few times; he carried the clubs on Tuesday for the minister from Eaglesham Parish Church, the Rev. D.L.Seath.

He even managed to get out onto the course on the first day of December 1936, and earn himself 3/6. However the snow fell at the end of the week, and there was no football on Saturday.

He had to wait a week before his next caddie.

Tuesday, 8 December 1936: *Mr Chalmbers' secretary; she gave me 4/6 for 12 holes.*

It was on this day that George heard the sensational news, and when he got home he noted it down in his diary.

Thursday, 10 December 1936: *I went up to Bonnyton Moor golf course after dinner. I got out, 2/6. The King (Edward) abdicated today.*

The following week he started work at MacIndoes Hen Farm, just across the road from Millerston. Mrs MacIndoe had called on his mother last week and kindly said, "I will give George a job till he gets on his feet again."

It had been a wonderful country existence in many ways throughout 1936: caddying up at the golf course, working on the farms, playing football every Saturday, going to the Old Boys' Association on Fridays, piano and dance lessons during the week, playing with the band at concerts, in theatres and church halls up and down the country, and of course going to the pictures. Along with the old year the events had somehow disappeared, and now he had a pony and a cart and he had to take them round the henhouses every morning.

Sunday, 27 December 1936: *Working in the morning from 8-12, then 5-3. I then went with the Old Boys' band to St George's Cross to play at the Service of Consecration of Officers.*

7

George went into another year with the view of taking part in everything that came his way. The O.B.A. held their annual parade on 14 April 1937 at the Argyll Theatre, Greenock. The programme included: Brass Bands, Boxing, Harmonica Band, and a mysterious play titled, 'The Ghost of Jerry Bundler'.

Neville Chamberlain on 28 May 1937, became the new British prime minister, and like all new prime minister's he promised many things.

Someone in the local area alerted George's father about a job down at Thornliebank. The Mond Nickel, an American Company, had many subsidiary companies up and down the country. The branch on the southside of the city, where they made metal tubes and propeller blades for engineering companies, was called Henry Wiggin & Co Ltd. So, as fate would have it, on 16 June 1937, George started work there at the Zenith Works.

He worked hard and became an active member in the Transport & General Workers Union. The number he was given was: 7/159. George liked it when the workers were united together in a cause, and like all good trade union members he believed that if the workforce stood together the unruly boss could, and would, be checked.

The general opinion among the workers was that man's inhumanity to man was caused by greed, and greed surfaced in the human race when an object of desire became the target for happiness.

For George the entitlement of working men and women to be able to negotiate their own terms and conditions had a human factor involved in it way beyond reason. His Christian upbringing fitted inside the spirit of the time like a hand does inside a glove. Some of the union men told him: "You must treat every man as your neighbour, your brother."

He liked the union, for the union stood up against injustice, and George felt at peace with the world when everyone was given their chance to take part in society. He worked away knowing the protection of the union, and before long a whole year had passed.

All over Europe, however, things were changing, and some people said that laissez-faire: freedom in commerce, had run its course as a popular doctrine. In Germany the people were now controlled by the National Socialist Workers Party, and the Nazi party made it clear that they wanted to get rid of all things non-Aryan.

The man who, people said, had reinvented the subconscious was over 80 now. The press still liked his ideas: 'Mental Derangement Traced To Sex Impulse,' but if truth be told still no one really knew what he was on about. The unconscious mind of man by the mid-thirties, for some reason, had been opened up again, and when people looked into it, after centuries of just looking out of it, many of them found concepts like: religion, the individual, the state, out of date.

It was hard to see where things were going in life, as well as where they were disappearing to. It was a time of great uncertainty. There was something in the air, something had ended, and something was just about to begin. Two opposing forces were about to face each other: democracy and dictatorship. And no one knew what was going to happen, or even who would win. In this obscure climate many people, especially politicians, simply went mad.

George felt profound things, like the unconscious mind, were best left alone. He felt that looking deep into the mind was like staring out into space. He felt life should be lived in the true spirit of things. He declared to his friends: "Start off on the right foot and you will not go far wrong."

One morning, at the beginning of the summer, a letter came through the door from Eric Low, the secretary of Eaglesham Amateurs Football Club. Eric invited George to come and join the team, but he also reminded him that although he had played only one game for his works team, Zenith F.C. after playing two games, for any amateur team, he could not thereafter change team in mid-season. George, liked the idea, and after a trial he joined Eaglesham Amateurs. The team played in a maroon and amber hoop strip. Ian, his brother, had once played for Eaglesham Amateurs before moving up the ranks to Junior teams like: Wishaw, Vale of Clyde and Rutherglen Glencairn.

George loved travelling up to Eaglesham on a Wednesday night for training and on a Saturday afternoon for the game. They say that Alexander Montgomery, the man who had planned the streets of the village, was stirred by an Italian/Swiss town that he had once seen. Eaglesham certainly had a continental feeling about it. The main streets of the town climbed up from the main road and faced each other, and down the middle lay a large common green.

The southside academics, when asked, declared that eagles and hamlets had been joined together to make up the name: Eaglesham. The village may have been neglected, but it still had an air of country romance about it. They were friendly people who lived there and they were kind. When the team played at home on a Saturday, George got the bus at 2 o'clock right outside his house at Millerston.

The town of Eaglesham lay quite high up, about 500 ft above

sea level, but it only took about ten minutes for the bus to climb the hill to get there. The old town of Eaglesham, demolished in 1769, must have been important; for an act of parliament was passed in the time of Charles the II, so that a weekly market could take place there. Handloom weaving had once been a steady industry, and there had also been a cotton mill at one time in the town. By 1901 there were just over a thousand souls living in the village, and by 1938 a few hundred had been added to that. There could have been more, but the railway had been barred from Eaglesham by the Gilmours; they did not want a direct link with the city people. The bus service was fairly regular now though: Monday to Saturday, about one every half an hour.

George was usually met off the bus by two young local lads: Donald McCabe and Stanley Smith. And as they all walked down in the direction of the plain two-storey country houses towards the town, the lads would carry his boots for him down to the dressing room. George would always give them a few coppers for their trouble.

Playfield, the football park, was situated opposite the Eglinton Arms Hotel. Around two o'clock on a Saturday after the village pubs came out: the Cross Keys and the Swan Inn, a crowd would usually gather outside the hotel. Then some of the men would make their way over to watch the game. Eaglesham had a good team that year and George played right-half alongside two excellent players: Cookie Cowan and Tommy Murphy.

On 18 January 1938, George even got a mention in the Daily Record newspaper, under the heading: More Hidden Talent On Junior Fields Than Comes To Light. 'The right half is being closely watched by several Junior clubs, but nothing will be done until Eaglesham is finished with their cup games.'

Even though he could hardly make out the scribble on the postcard that was sent to him, 13 July 1938: 'Bring boots if possible', George went along for a trial with Maryhill Hibernian

F.C. at Kelvinvale Park at 7.30. However, after giving it some thought he stayed with Eaglesham Amateurs.

That summer in the middle of August, George and a few of the lads from the work went to Douglas, in the Isle of Man. Many of them had been there before on holiday. So George and his friends every night before they hit the town would sit outside their boarding house and make some music. George played the mouth organ, someone bashed a tray, and someone else blew a trombone. What a racket! They had a great time.

In 1938 the civil war in Spain, between left and right forces, continued, and Germany assisted the right wing movement in Spain. To many this seemed like a dress rehearsal for something else. In early March 1938, German troops had crossed the border into Austria: the Anschluss. Chamberlain and the leaders of the other countries, France and Italy, met the German Chancellor, Herr Hitler, in September, in Munich. The leaders of Britain, France, and Italy tried to avoid any disagreements with him. They eventually agreed that Germany could go into the Sudetenland, excusing themselves by saying to the press that it was mainly Germans living there.

So on 1 October 1938, Germany annexed the Sudetenland, Czechoslovakia. Would Herr Hitler be happy with this? Would Fascism peter out? Would the Fascists now stop harassing the Jews? A month later the night of broken glass, Kristallnacht, took place and a thousand Jews were rounded up. As if to follow suit, Italy on the 10 November 1938, passed anti-Semitic laws. No one at the end of the year, if truth be told, felt very confident about going into 1939. All the dark signs pointed to war.

8

Youth movements were all the rage all over Europe at this time. George loved running, so he joined Overlee Amateurs Athletic Club. His favourite runner was P Nurmi the famous Finish runner. Fortunately for him the Mond Nickel Company, where he worked, liked promoting sports, and they had recreational facilities for their workers. Every year they held sports meetings up and down Britain with other subsidiary companies.

On 15th July 1939, George travelled to the Howley Grange, Birmingham, to take part in the Stanley Challenge Cup. He came second in event No 12, the long jump, with a jump of 18ft, but better luck followed; for at 4.25 that afternoon, in event No 18, he won the hundred yards flat handicap in 10.6 seconds. After the race George was presented with a beautiful crystal table lamp.

This may have been a time of great uncertainty, but George, Archie Shaw, and Tony Equi, the son of the cafe owner at Busby, were all young men, and they all fancied going abroad for the first time in their lives. They talked about it non-stop whenever they met. It is true to say that not many people they knew had ever been abroad, but this did not worry them. Tony suggested Italy, and for months they saved up their hard earned cash. Unfortunately, at the end of the summer Toni could not travel and had to pull out leaving only Archie and George to make the trip.

George, when the great day came, looked at his ticket, World Travel Service, 5 August 1939. Inside the wallet he noticed there was a funny drawing of a foreign railway man with a grand moustache. The man was running along the platform waving a cap, and holding onto a flag: 'Cook's Holidays by Special Train'. Then he read all the information inside the little brochure.

They had to get a train to London and then depart from Cannon Street by 20.00, arrive at Dover 21.46. depart from Dover at 22.10, arrive Ostend at 1.30. Then they were to board a Swiss special train, Ostend to Lucerne that would pass through Jemelle, Arlon Thionville, Metz.

'Luncheon can be obtained in the restaurant car (4/6 including gratuities).'

Then it was on to Strasbourg, Basle, Lucerne, Bellinzona, Lugano, Chiasso, Milan, then to Bologna. They should finally arrive in Rome at 17.50.

When they crossed the Alps, George sent a postcard of Lido mit Pilatus back home:

Here we are in Switzerland on the last stage of our journey. We had a good crossing of the Channel, and I am feeling fine. Cheerio - weather lovely.

And what a fabulous holiday they had! The lads tasted strange foods. They met young foreign ladies, and people from all over the world. They even met someone from Cramlington, Northumberland: David Scurfield.

George took lots of pictures, for everywhere they went he took his camera with him. He took pictures of curious little fishing boats making their way into the harbour in Osten, and some pictures of an open air stall selling melons in Ostia; but when they got to the Eternal City they were so many fabulous things to see he nearly ran out of film: the Trevi fountain; the policeman directing the traffic, dressed from head to foot in white, standing in the middle of the road on top of a circular raised platform; the beautiful La carrozza a cavalli taking people around the city; the Monument to Victor Emanuel II, built in 1574; and the former summer residence of the Popes now the residence of the Royal family.

They observed all the famous places in the time they were there: the Coliseum, built in AD 107, where they had once put lions in an arena along with the Christians; the Temple of the Vesta; the Tomb of Cecilia Metalla; the Pyramid of Caius Cestius; the Roman Forum; the Arch of Titus; the Ancient Appian Road; the Arch of Constantine; and the statue of Moses by Michealangelo.

George, before departing from Italy took a picture late one night of the balcony where Mussolini made his famous speeches from. They returned to British shores on the Prince Leopold ship at the end of August that summer, and the one thing that stuck in their minds was the amount of troops that they had seen moving about on trains all over Europe. In fact when they got back they remembered the fascist posters, militant slogans, and political propaganda, they had seen on walls all over Italy.

On 3 September 1939, about a week after they got back from Italy, at 11 o'clock in the morning, Britain declared war on Germany, and at 5 o'clock in the evening France declared war on Germany. The grounds for this war, like all other wars, will no doubt keep academics busy for years to come: the unfair Treaty of Versailles, more living space for all Germans, a belief in the right to conquer and change; however having said that no matter what reasons came to light, the nation was stunned, for Great Britain was now at war with Germany.

The Premier said, 4 September 1939: "We fight against evil things - brute force, bad faith, injustice, oppression, and persecution - and against them I am certain that the right will prevail."

The war came home to many people north of the border on the same day that the prime minister's statement was reported in the press: 'Glasgow Liner Torpedoed 200 miles west of the Hebrides.' It was also conveyed in print that Germans and Austrians, who did not intend to leave the country, were to report to the police.

The thought of conflict in Europe overwhelmed most people, but some were cock-a-hoop; for some people felt a modern pogrom of medieval Europe would sort things out. Some academics even said that international capitalism was to blame; others said that it was the fault of the Jews. Most folk, however, were just totally baffled and stunned, and they prayed hoping that hostilities would end soon - hopefully before the end of the year.

The accepted history of events went something like this: Hitler, the Nazi leader, had announced in 1935 a programme of rearmament, this had been forbidden by the Versailles treaty. The first sign of trouble came when Germany re-entered the demilitarized zone of the Rhineland; this had been forbidden. Then at 10pm on 12 March 1938, Germany annexed part of Austria. On 1 October 1938, Germany seized part of Czechoslovakia. The German leadership declared that this was justified, because many German citizens were living in these countries.

To many people Hitler had a dream of an old Germany before the defeat of Austria by Prussia. The British by September 1938 had reached a serious of agreements with Germany; they thought that Hitler would be satisfied with his gains, and Europe could be a peaceful nation once again. But Hitler wanted Danzig returned to the German people, and so after an agreement was reached with the Russians to divide Poland, on 1 September 1939, Germany marched into Poland.

The first sign of trouble came when Germany re-entered the demilitarized zone of the Rhineland; this had been forbidden.

The bible said there would be wars. It is written in Matthew 24:6

And when ye shall hear of wars and rumours of wars, be ye not troubled: for such things must needs be; but the end shall not be yet.

This was very hard to understand. War seemed to come out of nowhere. People were just going about their business, then all of a sudden all hell was let loose. People had to flee. War it was said brought out the best and the worst in people. People had to do things they could hardly imagine before the conflict.

The family during the troubled year of 1939 moved from Millerston, just down the road to Busby, to one of the new house's there, and for the first time mum had a real kitchen. Just around this time she heard about a woman whom she used to work for, apparently she was leaving the area. The woman was selling some paintings. So to decorate the walls, just like the rich, she bought two paintings from her; both signed by Victor Noble Rainbird, titled: Le Harve, and In Old Rouen.

When George looked out of his window from his new home at 19 Hawthorn Road, over the clubhouse of the nine hole golf course, he knew that central Europe lay some where over there, on the left hand side, in the direction where the sun came up every morning. Sometimes he would just stare and wonder. Then he would gaze back up towards Eaglesham.

It is true to say that, no matter where you lived in Britain at this time, it was hard to understand the reasons that lay behind the events that had just taken place way out there in the world.

George like everyone else felt that after an ultimatum had been issued against Germany, they surely knew what they were doing when they invaded another country - surely they realized the consequences.

George and Ian at Gulane B.B. camp 1934.

George with Finlayson's horse 1935.

Common Riding at Langholm 1933.

*The Bells, the Andersons,
and the Walkers at Langholm 1933.*

George with his mother, aunt Isable, uncle Matt, Walter and George Bell. 1935.

Three sisters from Langholm.

Davy Shaw and George,
working hard on Renfrew's Farm.

At Rothesay: George, John Ross,
Ian, Wullie Young.

World tour photo 1939: George and his great friend Archie Shaw.

The lads make it to the Eternal City.

Zenith works.
George with Peggy Clark, Ray Jackson, T Begbie.

The band in full swing outside boarding house,
Isle of Man, 1938.

1938 Eaglesham half-back line:
T Murphy, George, and Cookie Cowan.

Mearns Amateurs F.C. 1942.

The Cartvale Amateurs 1939.

George wins a beautiful crystal bowl at Birmingham 1939.

At this time it was natural for people to ask themselves, "Why have things got to this stage? Will this war last as long as the last war? Will peace follow war? Is it to late for peace?"

That month, September 1939, King George VI gave assent to the National Registration Bill; this act gave the government control over labour and identity cards. The radio programmes were constantly interrupted with bulletins about the war. People were told that it was an offence not to obey the blackout regulations. The pubs, restaurants, and hotels, had to shut at 8pm. An act from 1916 made it possible for people to get hitched quickly. Down at Clarkston Toll, opposite to where George had once stayed at Rowallandale, a siren was set up on top of the police station, and an air-raid warden was appointed for the area.

The local paper in the spirit of the times informed the people what was happening: 'On both sides of the River Cart the local home guards are now two or three times weekly seen to be putting in good solid training. The men are enthusiastic and respond well to their instructors, who are pleased with the progress being made, make no mistake about it when the emergency arises our local home guard will not be found wanting.'

All the national newspapers from beginning to end had huge battle headlines and true stories from the countries now at war. Even during the phoney war sport took a back seat, and only after some discussion did the cinemas and theatres stay open.

One piece of news though on 9 September 1939, seemed to slip into the war edition of the paper George's mother bought every day without anyone noticing it: there had been a strong earthquake in the little town of Monte Cassino, in Italy. The story looked so strange around all those battle headlines.

At the end of the month the Polish nation surrendered, and the first pictures of troops landing in France were published. Mind you the Italians were staying out of it, and the Soviets were reported to be staying out of it too. King George signed a proclamation saying that all men between 20 and 22 were now available for conscription. Food looked likely to be rationed next month.

A strange story appeared in a national newspaper saying that a concentration camp had been set up in Germany, and that people were being tortured there. The only bit of good news for George in October 1939, was that a truce had been called between Harry Roy and the B.B.C. over the playlist, and Harry should be back on the Radio soon.

In a beer cellar in Munich, 8 November 1939, someone tried to kill Hitler, but luck was not on his side and the Fuhrer escaped. Then out of the blue, taking advantage of the political situation, Russia invaded Finland. The headings on every page were now all about boats being sunk and aircraft being shot out of the sky.

When the last month of the year came along in 1939, everyone in the country knew that Christmas this year would be different from the others they had known in the past.

It was reported in a magazine at the beginning of the year that 1,315 fewer books were published in 1939 than the year before, however it was also reported that political books were on the increase. I guess the readers must have been trying to work out what the politicians were up to. Some of the books soon to be published in January 1940, had very exciting titles indeed: The Germans and the Jews; These Germans; Inside The Gestapo; How to Conquer Hitler; My Part In Germany; Sound And Fuehrer.

George's pal Archie Shaw had lodgings down at Holmhead Place, Cathcart, and George saw the new year in there. He left the flat at 4 am in the morning, and was lucky to get a lift back up to Clarkston Toll. And as George walked home that night, back to 19 Hawthorn Road, Busby, he like everyone else in the country wondered what lay ahead of him in a world now at war.

9

It was announced in the press in January 1940, in between huge photographs of ships going down, that food would soon be rationed. Germany had threatened Sweden, and conscription now extended to all young men between the ages of 20-27, in Great Britain.

George wanted to go to war and do his bit, but the authorities had told him he was exempt. The factory, Henry Wiggin & Co Ltd, where he worked at Thornliebank was now involved in the production of armaments for the war effort. This news at the beginning of the year made him fed up; for all his pals were joining up and doing their bit - but what could he do? He thought about it all the time, but there was nothing he could do except go back to work with all the workers on 2 January 1940.

Friday, 5 January 1940: *I was working till 9pm tonight. We had an A.R.P. demonstration, at our work today. My wage was £2.7.1.*

Yes, even though the country was at war life simply had to go on, and playing football cheered the lads up no end. The following Saturday George played for the local team, Cartvale Amateurs, against his old team Eaglesham Amateurs, the score 1-1.

On Thursday, 18 January 1940, the snow fell during the night and continued right through the weekend. It became extremely cold; so much so that the following week there was nothing but frozen and burst pipes everywhere. Everyone on the southside of Glasgow found it difficult walking to work through the deep snow.

Monday, 29 January 1940: *Working till 9pm. No buses came down from Eaglesham today, for the snow has blocked the road. The papers say it is the heaviest snow fall in living memory.*

One night, George, in the middle of February 1940, went with a friend dancing to the Dixon Halls, Glasgow. He knew the works dance would take place at the beginning of March, next month, and he wanted to get some practice in, "Yes, you have got to grab the chance whenever it comes along," was the idea.

He agreed to play centre half for the works team on Saturday, 24 February 1940: Zenith Amateurs 0 v 2 Royal Technical College. And just like last year, and the year before that, and the year before that, every Sunday he went along to Greenbank church and then went for a walk in the country in the afternoon.

Every day now, just like it had during the Great War, the papers were full of huge maps of Western Europe; they appeared on the front and back pages, along with stories predicting the forthcoming events. The stories were very interesting indeed; one journalist reckoned that Stalin and Hitler had some kind of agreement. The Swedes were not letting any army go through their country - even if it were to fight the Boche. The Jews and Arabs were joining up to fight against Fascism. Germany by this time had stopped all movement over its border. Jack Kennedy the U.S. Ambassador viewed that America intended to stay out of the conflict.

The works dance, 2 March 1940, in the Prince of Wales Hall, went well. And the following day, when he got the chance, George went to the General Post Office in town and bought 3% War Loan Bonds to help the war effort. On his way into town he bought a paper. In the paper that very same day, he noticed above the heading: Officer's Bride, a familiar figure.

When he got back from town he showed the photograph to his mother, "This is Dr Henderson, the man who stitched my head when I split it open last year while playing football at Overlee Park," and as he handed her the paper, he added, "Look the good doctor got married yesterday."

Mum had some good news too, for she had bought another lovely oil painting from an old lady in the church who stayed at Clarkston. The painting was inside a fancy gilt-edged frame, and it had been painted by David Fulton, and was titled: Kyles of Bute from Kames. The original painting really did look something when it was put up on the wall.

George for most of the month worked late till 9pm at the factory, 15 March 1940: *This has been a very busy week for us, and I am feeling very tired. My wage £3-14-9.*

George did not play football that Saturday, instead he went into town and bought a mute for his cornet 8/6.

Thankfully the Easter holidays came round and they stopped work on Friday, 22 March 1940. George and his mother left Glasgow for Langholm at 10 am on Saturday. They arrived down in the Muckle Toon around 3pm.

His cousin Walter had joined the Royal Navy and some of his friends had already joined the K.O.S.B. This dilemma about having to work at home while others were going abroad unsettled George; however everyone enjoyed the weekend and they returned to Glasgow at 6.45 on Monday.

At the end of that week George got the chance to say something about it at work.

Thursday, 28 March 1940: *Mr Stott my boss at work was speaking to me about registering, I said I didn't want to be exempt. He hoped things would work out and that he too could go and do his bit.*

Aunty Bell and cousin Walter repaid them with a visit the following week. They arrived from Langholm at 10.30 on the last Friday of the month. And on Saturday, 30 March 1940,

George, his father, and Walter all went to the football, at Cathkin Park, to see Third Lanark 2 v 1 St Mirren. Aunty Bell and George's mother met them in town after the match, and they all had tea at Peacock's restaurant in the city centre. Then Walter and George went to the Empire at night to see: 'Roll Out The Barrel'.

In April 1940, it seemed the Phoney War was not so phoney after all, for the first house in Britain had been bombed. And according to press reports the economic blockade of Germany was going to be a futile gesture.

The weather in the early part of the month, however, was not too bad and whenever he got the chance George worked in the garden at the front of 19 Hawthorn Road, and at night he worked down at the factory.

Eaglesham Amateurs could not get a team together, because of all the young men being called up, so for the rest of the season George decided to play for the Cartvale Amateurs.

On the first Saturday of the month, after playing football for the local team, against Craigton - they had only nine men - he tried again to do his bit. At 5.30 he went into town to the recruiting agency. The attractive poster for the R.A.F. on the wall inside the building had a man standing tall in a flight jacket. The man was holding his helmet under his arm, and was shielding his eyes from the sun. The poster read: There's a place for you in the R.A.F.

Saturday, 6 April 1940: *Today I registered for Military Service with the 25 year olds. They asked me what I wanted? I said the R.A.F. The manager at the work gave me a form which shows that I am in a government job, but I asked him to be released as I feel I want to go to war.*

A few days later George read that the Germans had swarmed over Denmark and Norway. Now he had to work right through the night at the factory, and if the crane broke down it became a long shift indeed. George did not like working outside on the crane, for it poured out smoke and the fumes gave him a sore head; however he had to do it.

Friday, 12 April 1940: *This was a busy day for me; a big wheel at the Draw Benches broke, and the fitters are going to work at it all night. So I left the work at 9.15pm went home and then returned at 11.23pm to work all night. We stopped for a meal at 2.30am.*

Saturday, 13 April 1940: *I managed to sleep from 7 till 8am, then I worked till 12 noon. I went home and had one and a half hour's sleep, and then went to Overlee Park and played left-half for the Cartvale Amateurs against Copland Waverly. We won 7-0. I felt remarkably fresh.*

By Wednesday, 17 April 1940, George had still not received a reply to his letter as regards joining up, so he sent a note to Mr Mellon via the office boy saying:

Sir, Would you be kind enough to inform me if the management have reached a decision in connection with my release for Military service?

Within 15 minutes a reply came back down to the shop floor, then Mr Mellon sent for George. He said in a friendly tone that Mr Graham wanted to see him upstairs in the office. When he got there Mr Graham said that without the works consent he could not join up, "I am afraid you're needed here at work, George, more than you are in the forces."

George tried to understand, but without his consent he could do nothing.

The following Saturday he played for the Cartvale Amateurs. They drew 2-2 in the cup against G.E.I. George hurt his knee and the doctor told him to rest it for a while, but he wanted to play in the replay.

People in Britain were now starting to wonder if Germany could invade Britain. There had been an article in the paper not long ago on this very question. On the continent an editor of an Italian newspaper figured that Italy would soon enter the war, but he did not say on which side - only that the war, which has fallen upon Norway, may fall upon Italy. Two days later in the national press there was some bad news for the ladies. The article appeared under the heading: 'Silk Stockings Soon To Be Rationed.'

At the beginning of May 1940, even though he came home tired the following day, George played in the replay of the cup. They won 2-1 and the Cartvale Amateurs went through to the semi-final of the Glasgow Amateur Cup.

Wednesday, 8 May 1940: *Davy Shaw and I went to the Election Meeting in Busby School Hall and heard the I.L.P. 'Stop The War' candidate, Miss Annie Maxton; her brother Jimmy Maxton also spoke.*

War report, 10 May 1940, Germany has invaded Holland and Belgium.

The factory workers had meant to stop for the Whitsun holidays, but leave was cancelled, for things were getting serious.

Saturday, 11 May 1940: *I went to town this afternoon and got measured for a new shirt at 10/6. When I was in town I saw lots of French soldiers, the Chasseurs Alpins, just back from Norway.*

The month of May had many significant developments: children were being evacuated from the south east of England to the coast. In all the national newspapers black arrows inside maps pointed from Germany towards France. And there was a change at the top of British politics: 'Chamberlain Quits, Churchill becomes Leader.' The war headings were all so solemn and surreal: 'The R.A.F. Attack's Germany; Luftwaffe Bomb Channel Ports; Germans Claim French 9th Army Defeated; British Expeditionary Force is Surrounded on French coast; An Evacuation of British, French, and Belgian Troops Takes Place From Dunkirk; Hitler summons Goebbels.'

The press think an announcement is due as regards the Italian question. Will Italy stay out of it? or Will she come in on the

German side? The Italian press say she is getting ready to fight - but who will she fight? 'Ships In The Med; Diplomats At The Vatican; Russians Warn The Duce To Stay Out Of It; Americans Told To Come Home; State Control Of Britain; French Towns Bombed.'

Tuesday, 21 May 1940, *I was playing tonight for the Cartvale Amateurs in the semi-final of the Cup. We left Busby at 7pm in a special bus for South Park, the Ground of Rutherglen Glencairn.*

Friday, 24 May 1940: *I was working till 9pm. The whole work has to be in at the weekend; this is because the situation is so grave.*

George now had to work most nights till 9pm, and sometimes it got him down.

Tuesday, 28 May 1940: *The British are retreating from Flanders. I do nothing but eat, sleep, and work these days.*

Thankfully winning the semi-final of the Amateur Cup at the end of May took his mind off the war. However, it did not last long for no word came through about their neighbour Donald Adair, Royal Artillery. He had been lost in France. Jessie Watson came round to George's house, at Hawthorn Road, asking if they had heard any news about him, but no one had heard anything.

The exceptionally hot weather in June 1940, brought the good people out onto the streets and everyone talked about the momentous events that were taking place on the other side of the channel: the evacuation at Dunkirk. One of the first soldiers, who had already returned from Flanders, reported in the paper, "It was hell!"

Yes, it was true a mighty German assault through the Ardennes had taken everyone by surprise, and now the whole of France was crying for help. The Americans may have publicly backed Britain and France, but they have not declared war on Germany yet. Everyone around the local area seemed to know someone over there in France. When he goes out George listens and talks just like everybody else, and he tries to understand the situation; for there has never been a time like this before.

A week after the evacuation at Dunkirk, 11 June 1940, Mussolini pops up and lo and behold the ex-journalist, turned gangster, declares war on the defeated Nations. Hitler of course sent him a note of thanks, 11 June 1940: "The German Army rejoices to be able to stand in the battle side by side with its Italian comrades." 22 June 1940, the Italians bomb Alexandria, Egypt.

The following Saturday George went down to the shows at Cathkin Park where he won a tumbler, a butter dish, and a vase at shooting; and on Sunday, after church, he went to St. Mungo's Halls again to see what his chances were of joining the R.A.F. The recruiting officer once again told him he could do nothing till the work released him.

On Monday, 24 June 1940, George sent a letter to Mr Graham, the Works Manager:

Dear Sir, A little while ago I had the pleasure of an interview with you regarding my request to be released for military service. It was a great disappointment to me, when you decided that you couldn't let me go. I thought I would gradually forget about it, but no, a day or two after the interview the longing returned to join the R.A.F. At that time I decided I would carry on working till Mr Bowman returned to work.

I think you could let me go now without putting the work to any great disadvantage; as for the argument that I will be wanted in the Despatch Department - have they not carried on without me for two months.

It pleased me very much when you said that I am quite a useful person in the work, but I say without boasting I will be far more useful in the fighting forces. I do hope you will alter your decision.

A few days later the letter that George had written to Mr Graham came back to him, and at the bottom of it he noticed some writing in black ink:

'I appreciate your ideas! You must understand, however, that I am not the best judge as to how your services should be employed. In the meantime you must remain at your job.'

The news that the local Cartvale Amateurs team had won the Glasgow Amateur Cup, seemed to lift spirits around the town; it restored a bit of sanity back into a world that had gone mad: 'War Hysteria in America; Luxury Goods Rationed at Home; Petain Orders French to Stop Fighting; Britain To Recognize du Gaulle As Leader Of The Free French.'

George wondered about his friend Tony who worked at the cafe at Busby, for they were starting to intern all the Italians in the city. Then one day he heard that he had been sent away to the Isle of Man.

Tuesday, 25 June 1940: *At 1am this morning we had our first Air Raid warning of the war. The sky was a mass of light with searchlights; there was no gunfire and no bombs dropped. We distinctively heard the drone of the German Bombers, but we didn't see them.*

The unprecedented events at this time in life changed everyone in one way or another for the rest of their lives, but somehow life - even though the pace of events in war seemed terrific - just went on at a normal pace.

George in the new spirit of the time walked to work the following Sunday morning, and as he walked down the familiar route passed Clarkston Toll towards Giffnock, even though the unthinkable had happened in the world, he could still rejoice in the good things of life.

Sunday, 30 June 1940: *I was working today. It was a lovely morning, I enjoyed the walk down to work, everything seemed so quiet and peaceful.*

Someone said something in the paper about the nation's favourite drink; it appeared tea was going to be rationed soon. The young women, however, in 1940, were not really worried about a tax on make-up, "We will pay up with a smile," they said.

On the other side of the world the people in the United States of America had no such shortages; however moral questions troubled them like: Should we stay out of it? or Should we jump in? The political animals in the States remained diffident; they did not want to do anything rash, "Let's wait and see what happens," they told the people.

George, after reading all about the war exploits of Max Aitken, wanted even more now to do his bit. When he had worked with the Daily Express, George had played in the same football team as the proprietor's son.

When the Battle of Britain started everyone in Britain knew that the Germans were not all that faraway now. They attacked convoys in the English Channel and bombed the Welsh docks. The enemy soon occupied the Channel Islands. There followed a period of quiet and then a German plane, just to remind everyone about the war, dropped its bombs at Govan, not all that far from Glasgow city centre, fortunately no one was killed. Then the activity seemed to increase.

Saturday, 20 July 1940: *We had an Air Raid early this morning. We were wakened at 1.30 by the sirens. I heard bombs being dropped in the distance. The all clear signal went at 2.40 am.*

At the end of July 1940, George, one evening went up to see Tommy Murphy and they arranged a social night for the presentation of medals for the football team. Then at the beginning of August they met again this time at George's house, 19 Hawthorn Road. George after the meeting telephoned and booked the Busby school hall, and then he phoned Jimmy Carabine, Third Lanark, to see if he would present the medals.

War report: The Italians have faced British troops in Somaliland, East Africa. The Pope has declared that he is going to be a lightning rod to keep the peace. Dog fights between British and German forces have been reported over the channel.

A massive air attack, 15 August 1940, by German planes. The Russians are staying neutral.

Aunt Agnes and Uncle Eddy arrive from Langholm, on the same day as the ceremony to the football team. All the lads before going to the social event head down to the local artist's studio, and there inside Tom Lindsay's house a picture is taken of the football team.

That night, 16 August 1940, a reporter from the local southside newspaper turns up and writes a piece for the weekly paper about the Cartvale Amateurs:

'Busby School Drill Hall was filled to capacity last Saturday evening when the above soccer village combine staged a social and dance to celebrate their dual triumph of last season, the winning of the Glasgow Amateur Cup and top place in the First Division of Glasgow and District Amateur League, the latter success without dropping a point. Mr George McLean a past president of the club, occupied the chair and was supported on the platform by Jimmy Carabine, Neil Dewar, and Sam Brown of the Third Lanark Club, and Mr William Garman senr. After extending a warm welcome to their honoured guests, the chairman went on to congratulate the club on the success of their efforts to keep the soccer flag flying throughout the difficulties of the present critical period. He then called upon James Carabine to present the trophies won by the club, and Jimmy, with a few well-chosen remarks, handed them over to Captain Jim Anderson amidst loud applause.

During the evening Neil Dewar and Sam Brown made some happy remarks anent their pleasure in attending the function and wished the Amateurs all future success.

The dance which followed was a great success with the ever-popular Bud Hopkins as M.C. The committee are due congratulations on the excellence of their arrangements and thanks are also due to Robert McGhie (janitor) for his helpful co-operation throughout what proved to be a memorable evening.'

When George went to work the following Monday, 26 August 1940, he found the Home Guard standing guard outside the factory gates. A blitz had taken place in London on Saturday evening and it had lasted all night. Things were obviously getting worse. It had even been suggested that all the children down south should now be sent to castles and strong houses up in the Highlands.

The Home Guard, as well as guarding factories and watching for enemy infiltration, made it known that they were on the lookout for volunteers for their organization. George could see that the men guarding the factory consisted mainly of ex-service men. He knew it was their job to spot enemy planes and patrol different areas around the village. George wondered if he should volunteer and help them in his spare time; however after much consideration, he told a friend, "No, I won't join them, because I don't want to be tied to anything which might keep me from joining the R.A.F."

Tommy Murphy and George organized a bus run to Ayr to celebrate the team winning the League and Cup. The bus left at 2.30 in the afternoon on Sunday, 1 September 1940, and arrived at the coastal town at 4.30. They had a fabulous day out at the seaside, and they returned home late that night; everyone really enjoyed themselves. During the week a full committee meeting took place in Tommy Murphy's house, and George accepted the position and took over as treasurer for the new season.

In the middle of the night, 18 September 1940, George's mother wakened him; for there were planes above, and Anti Aircraft fire could be heard in the distance. She had read in the newspaper last week - like everyone else - that the invasion of Britain could take place this week.

18 September 1940: *Early this morning at 1am the sirens sounded. At 2am they gave the all clear. I heard a plane; I heard bombs drop at about 2.30. There were four alarms during the night. The last at 5.am.*

As usual the football season started on 5 October 1940, and right at the beginning of the new term George and the rest of the committee organize a dance for the players' girlfriends and wives. The committee will again meet, all going well, every Thursday night.

Thursday, 3 October 1940: *We held a committee meeting in Tommy Murphy's house to pick a team for Saturday. This is the start of the new season. Jimmy Steele was present, he is home on leave from Berwick. Jimmy is in the K.O.S.B.*

The workers in the factories had to keep up their strength, and one Friday, as he stood waiting for his wages, George is handed a small bottle of vitamin tablets.

Friday, 1 November 1940: *We received a small box of 'Adexolin' capsules along with our wages tonight. The firm is supplying them they contain vitamins. There are 14 in the box and we have to take one every day. My wage £3-17-8. plus 7/6 for Sunday.*

The nights were fairly drawing in once again, but even with all this activity going on no one could by the end of the year say that they were used to the feeling of being at war.

Monday, 4 November 1940: *We had an air Raid tonight from 7.20 till 9.30. We could hear the planes flying at a great height. The A.A. opened up on them. Bombs were dropped in Burnside. Mrs McAdam was so frightened that she came into our house till the all clear.*

George read in the paper that the shops were to shut at 6pm until the spring. He also read about how Coventry had been blitzed and how the people had cried back: "Bomb Back Heavy!" On the world stage Hitler had the Russian Foreign Minister Molotov as a guest, and closer to home another casualty was recorded.

Wednesday, 13 November 1940: *Colin Castle was killed today. He was in the R.A.F.*

To get away from it all George goes to the pictures with Betty, a local girl. He met her coming up the road on Tuesday, after work, and fixed a date for Thursday.

Friday, 29 November 1940, *I was working till 9pm tonight. There was an Air Raid warning from 6.30am till 7.10am.*

Davy Shaw, now stationed at Perth, paid George a visit although during the stay he told George, "I expect to get shifted next week."

At the beginning of the last month of the year, George and Alex McLean go to the Kingston Hall dancing, it is mainly old time dancing there, but they enjoy it.

Sunday 15 December 1940: *I was working all day. I made up a parcel to send to Peter Park, who is in the R.E. at Winchester. I sent 40 cigarettes, a tube of shaving cream, and a cake.*

Some bright spark working in the ministry suggested to the people that they should eat more mutton. Meanwhile, Cadburys, the chocolate people, put an apology in the paper as regards the rationing of chocolate.

Lord Lothian the ambassador to America one day around this time looked into the future and reckoned: "Britain can win in a year." Churchill on the other hand warned the people in his Christmas address about the threat of invasion. Down at the factory life went on as usual and people everywhere just got on with things as best they could.

Friday, 20 December 1940: *Donald Fergusson left the work tonight to get married. They hurled him round on a barrow. The bombers were overhead tonight, the warning was from 8.30-9.10pm. The aeroplanes passed overhead. There was some A.A. fire and bombs dropped; another alarm went from 12.30 till 1am.*

10

I suppose the year 1941, taking everything into account, got off to a reasonable start for those on the side of democracy: Franklin D. Roosevelt sent a bill, Lend Lease, 6 January 1941, to Congress - this would surely help Britain.

However, newspapers in Germany imply that Britain is going to invade Eire soon. The papers in the United States suggest that the Germans are just waiting for the right weather conditions to invade Britain.

If truth be told no one knows what is going on. The cigar smoking Churchill at the beginning of the year visits Glasgow. Meanwhile, just down the road from where George stays a woman is murdered at Clarkston.

On the war front the Royal Navy hammers North Africa day and night, and on the land many battles are fought. The Allies, in late January 1941, take Tobruk from the Axis, and then in February 1941, they take Benghazi; the British deal with the Italians in Libya, Eritrea, and Ethiopia. Rommel, fresh from victories in France, shows up in the Libyan desert in February 1941. At the end of February Franco kindly tells Hitler: "I stand today already at your side entirely and decidedly at your disposal."

The following month the Germans admit occupation of Bulgaria. The Germans attack the West of Scotland, 14 March 1941, hitting hospitals, tenements and office blocks. The R.A.F continues to Bomb Bremen and other German cities. With all the bombs that are being dropped is it any wonder that people all over the world are starting to question if Britain can hold out. A general in the U.S. army, declares in a British newspaper: "Germany will invade Britain in either April or May this year." Malta comes under attack in May, and closer to home Clydebank, on the other side of the city from where George lives, is blitzed, along with several other British cities.

The Germans, in the spring of 1941, swarm over Yugoslavia and Greece - the Italians have been struggling in Greece since October last year - and Britain is propelled from Europe once again. In the desert the Germans win many victories, but are repulsed at Tobruk.

Nearer to home bombs are being dropped all over the place - even one in the Busby Glen. And a rumour is going round the village of Busby about a plane crash. The plane was said to have crashed on Saturday night up near the Windmill Farm, not far from the Floors Road. George knew the farm quite well and, like everyone else in the area, called it the Winnall farm; in fact Davie Shaw's father-in-law worked there on the farm.

A few days later on Tuesday, 13 May 1941, George as usual picks up the morning paper before going to work and, after staring at the photograph of the German officer on the front page, he reads the banner heading: 'Deputy Fuhrer Gives Himself Up.'

He could hardly believe it: for the plane that had crashed on Saturday night, half-way between Eaglesham and Mearns, was the one carrying the Deputy Leader of the Nazi Party, Rudolf Hess. George stares at the paper again, then he reads about how Rudolf Hess had parachuted down from the dark blue sky from a two-seater fighter- bomber, Messerschmitt ME110, on Saturday night.

The Deputy Fuhrer, who had learnt to fly during the First World War, had by all accounts left Germany at 6pm. The report said that the plane had crashed at 11-15pm on the same night about 500 yards from a cottage where a farm worker lived. Apparently, the plane had circled the cottage many times.

George did not know the farm worker in question, but he knew the farmer and his wife. It was a strange thing all together; in fact the farm worker when he first heard the noise had thought there were about five planes up there. However, when he looked out of the cottage window he saw a parachute coming down from the sky and land right in the middle of his field. The man said that the Messerschmitt plane crashed just at the moment the pilot landed, and immediately burst into flames. The farm-worker and his mother then brought the pilot into the cottage. His mother asked him if he was a German. Then seeing him hurt, she asked him if he wanted a cup of tea. The pilot answered her like a gentleman, but took only a cup of water. The pilot then sat down and showed them some photographs of his son. He told the ploughman that his name was Alfred Horn.

Presently, a Home Guard arrived up at the cottage. The pilot asked him if he was British. The Home Guard asked him where he had come from. The German pilot told him Munich. A few other soldiers arrived. Then after some interesting minutes had passed, the German pilot bowed at the farm-worker and his mother, then he left the cottage with the soldiers.

There may have been excitement around the villages of Busby, Eaglesham and Mearns, before the announcement in the press about the Deputy Fuhrer landing on the southside of Glasgow, but now the place was absolutely buzzing. The next day some of the locals said that Hess had been taken to the Girls Club Hall at Hawthorn Road, Busby, just round the corner from where George stayed.

Naturally, people started to wonder if Hess had been trying out some secret plane and had been blown off course. The press said that the Deputy Fuhrer wanted to speak to the Duke of

Hamilton, at Dungavel. Did he have a peace plan with him? It wasn't long till rumours abounded all over the place. Was the Deputy Leader of the Nazi Party on a secret mission? Did he have some important news on him for the Prime Minister? Did he have any documents on him that would help the Allies? Had he defected?

The whole country could not believe it. The castle in Eaglesham owned by someone called Gilmour right enough had a similar style to the one the Duke of Hamilton stayed in. Whatever he had, or had not come for, the Deputy Fuhrer was duly taken away into Glasgow, and eventually, someone said, up to the Bar L: Barlinnie prison.

Hess probably thought that he had reached his destination, and bailed out at the right spot. Apparently, the plane had come north so as to miss the air defences, and it had circled the castle many times before crashing. Hitler must have gone off his head when he heard what Rudolf had been up to; mind you everything considered it was a miracle that Hess made it to Scotland in a twomotored plane.

The strange thing about the whole incident was that the plane came down on the edge of the only exclusive Jewish golf course in the country: Bonnyton Moor. Imagine if the Deputy Fuhrer had hidden all night in a field nearby, and in the morning wandered up to the clubhouse, "Good morning gentlemen, I have come to give myself up, I am looking for the Duke of Hamilton; I must speak to him, it is very important for both our countries..."

George, because of all the football he had played, was told by the doctor that he had to go in and get a cartilage operation. When he was in Hairmyers Hospital, which was not that far away from Busby, he met Corporal Jonny Cairns, from Paisley, and Lynall Lloyd, from Wales. Jonny had been wounded in the war and Lynall had fallen off his motorbike. Lynall, who everyone called Taffy, had also fallen in love, and in the spirit of the time he was married in hospital. George also met a Lancashire fusilier and a corporal Cliff Sykes.

They all had great fun while waiting for treatment, laughing and joking, with sister Kellar, and nurse Stein, and nurse Young; and when Lynall and Jonny got better, George invited them down to Busby to meet his folks.

War report: the first ever large-scale airborne invasion gets underway, 21 May 1941, the Germans invade Crete from the sky. The British battle cruiser the Hood is sunk off Greenland, then a few days later the Bismarck follows her to the bottom of the ocean.

At the beginning of June 1941, Alexandria is pounded, 100 are people killed, and at the end of the month, 22 June 1941, Germany launches Operation Barbarossa. The operation is named after a crusading German emperor of the middle ages. The Germans then sweep into western Russia and vast numbers of Soviet prisoners are taken. On the streets of Britain people are astounded, they say that this campaign will be the most decisive of the war. If Hitler wins the war in the East - it could take decades to defeat him.

In the city centre of Glasgow, 4 July 1941 the American flag is hoisted up on top of an office in the middle of town; this of course has a great effect on anyone passing by. The people, while wondering about freedom and justice, hope and pray that the Americans will enter the war soon. At the end of July 1941, Finland declares war on Russia. One day Franco the Spanish leader gazed into the future and said: "The Allies have already lost!" but he did not declare war on anyone.

The following month an article appears in the morning paper saying that Hess had been part of a secret service plot. On 11 August 1941, Churchill and Roosevelt meet and both countries sign the Atlantic Charter: a pact between a country at war and one at peace with a view to ending Nazi rule in Europe. The two men plan for victory. Mussolini, September 1941, is faced with a demand from the Germans to extend martial law, and the Germans want their advisers to sit on Italian courts.

Meanwhile, in another part of the world, Marshal Voroshilov tells the people of Leningrad to defend the city to the last man against the Germans. The reports, coming back home in October 1941, did not look good for the Russians, for the Germans were not all that far from Moscow. What will happen if Russia is conquered? Will the Germans then try to make peace with the Allies? This would suit the evildoers; for their next target would surely be Britain. However, early in November 1941, the German attack is halted, and by the end of the month the Red Army retakes Rostov. Things appear to be changing.

Lord Halifax arrives in New York, 4 November 1941, to promote the British cause. And just before going into a meeting in the city centre a woman pelts him with an egg, and shouts: "Fight your own wars!"

News comes through at the end of November 1941, that the British Eighth Army are opening up an offensive in Libya.

Hitler, in December 1941, could only retreat and abandon the German offensive towards Moscow. The days of the week had just reached the Sabbath when out of the blue the Japanese drop bombs onto American ships at Pearl Harbour. The Americans are in.

Hitler and Mussolini, 11 December 1941, declare war on America. America then declares war on Germany and Italy. Now the war picture is clear: The British Empire, the Soviet Union, and the United States, are against Germany, Italy, and Japan; although the Soviet Union, for some reason, do not declare war on Japan, but then again everyone understands, for words and deeds are complicated things in war. Japan said that she had been pushed into the conflict: for America has placed an embargo on her products. She also says that she will win the war against China.

Christmas approaches and the birth of Jesus is celebrated once again; and as another year ends everyone tries to understand the events that have just taken place, but for the majority of those that wonder, reason has no logic - only suffering.

11

The American people are no longer caught between isolation and war; the people kick off the new year, 1942, by getting behind their president. The Americans get into the war mood, and soon all the papers in Britain are full of American slang: 'Let's get over there and get the job done. Yes, sir, the yanks will do the business!'

The Japanese looking for more living space set their sights on the territory of foreign empires. They soon grab Manila, and in the middle of the first month they enter the Dutch East Indies, Kuala Lumpur capital of Malaya, and then Burma from Thailand; towards the end of the month they land at Balikpapan.

Rommell on the 21 January 1942, launches a counter attack, and soon his troops recapture Benghazi. The bombs seemed to have stopped over Britain; however the R.A.F. continue to drop bombs over enemy territory throughout Europe.

Allied troops refuse to give in at Singapore; but on 15 February 1942, they surrender to the Japanese because of the lack of food, petrol and ammunition. The Australian Prime Minister calls it: "Australia's Dunkirk." The Japanese land on Java, Indonesia, at the end of the month.

In Britain in March 1942, the government warns racketeers that they will be dealt with severely. The newspapers are further reduced in size because of the war. The small editions are now full of reports of landings by Japanese troops, here and there in the East. The Japs now occupy Batavia. Meanwhile, the Australians warn the Japs that they will bushfire their own lands if the Japs invade their country. Ships on their way to Malta come under attack.

In April 1942, Stafford Cripps, tried to get things sorted out in India, and someone asked Mahatma Gandhi, the Indian Guru, to say a few words as regards the war raging in the East. Gandhi replied, "I would let the Japanese land and fight them by non-violence." Finally the Japanese capture Bataan, the largest surrender of U.S. soldiers to date.

Lord Beverbrook, around this time, trying to keep spirits up, stuck his neck out and, in an optimistic tone, said, "I reckon the war could be settled this year."

A joint report, from high command in London and Washington, hinted that a second front could be opening up soon in Italy. Hitler must have had the same idea in mind too; for he met Mussolini at the beginning of May, and word got out that thousands of Germans were to be sent to Italy.

Rumours seemed to be everywhere: "The Japs are ready to invade Russia," said a US journalist in a British paper.

There will be no let up for the workers back home; the government announces a 52-hour working week. The people on both sides of the conflict are kept up-to-date by film, radio, and newspaper reports; propaganda sets the tone.

A battle takes place just off Midway Island in the Pacific at the beginning of June between the U.S. and the Japanese. The Japanese retreat and with heavy losses. Tobruk is taken by the German African Corp, 21 June 1942. R.A.F. Bombers continue with raids over Germany.

The B.B.C. warn Germany that all war towns will be razed to the ground. Il Duce turns up at the coastal town of Derna and waits there; apparently he wants to march into Cairo like some ancient god.

At the beginning of July 1942 the British hold El Alamein. In Russia, Svestopool falls to the Germans. And an article appears in the morning paper inviting British families to ask an American home for tea. Bastille day in France is celebrated and some brave people march in search of liberation. The Germans recapture Rostov, at the end of the month.

In the summer of 1942, George, one morning, received a telegram from Third Lanark Football Club, then some postcards followed. One of the cards read: 'Trial at Cathkin Park, kick off 7.30, meet at pavilion 7pm, bring boots.' He also received a letter from his dad's old club Mearns Amateurs, and from Bedlay Juniors. George, after weighing up all his options, decides to join Mearns Amateurs.

In August 1942, after some more Jews are rounded up in Paris, a British organization claims that a million Jews have already been killed in Europe. Churchill arrives in Moscow to discuss the war with Stalin. And in the desert Alexander replaces Auchinleck as Commander in Chief. The first U.S. bombing raid takes place over Europe.

The Germans launch a massive attack on Stalingrad at the beginning of September 1942. Food riots in Hungary. In Britain letter writers are asked to write on both sides of the paper to save any waste. A great number of people are arrested in Paris after a grenade attack in the city.

The war rages on in the East; the Japanese are pushed back by the Australians at New Guinea in the second week of October 1942. The British government announces that Rudolf Hess will be tried at the end of the war. Second battle of El Alamein gets under way.

Rommel retreats in early November 1942, and a German underground station reports that Rommel has left the desert and is now in Italy; and from then on people report sightings of him all over the place.

A report comes out of America saying that Italy will be blitzed soon. The Gestapo, afraid of no one, pours more troops into Italy. Italian radio reports of large-scale evacuation of cities: Turin, Genoa, and Milan. Russian forces push out of Stalingrad.

Marseilles is occupied by Nazi forces in December 1942. A report from America claims that the Italian army may mutiny soon, and that many civilians are leaving their homes to avoid R.A.F. bombing raids. Rommel retreats as Eighth army continues to advance. The war rages on in the East.

The war as 1942 ends seems more and more like some nasty disease as it spreads here and there all over Europe. People everywhere start to wonder: "How long will it take to bring the opposing factions together again in peace and harmony?"

12

War report: at the beginning of 1943 the Germans and their Axis partners retreat from Russia. This time Hitler has no good news, or excuses, for the people of Germany. With the Allies in control of north-west Africa, the war as far as the press is concerned seems to be heading in the right direction. American bombers, for the first time, bomb German cities.

George, in the spring of 1943, receives a letter from a government office in Glasgow indicating that he will be called up soon. Not one to hang about he writes a letter into the March edition of the Forest Magazine. The magazine has been set up so that companies can correspond under different tree names and not give any information away to the enemy.

With the war in its fourth year, I don't think my call up can be delayed much longer, so I am taking this opportunity of giving my views on the subject.

My mind flies back to that fateful day in September 1939, when war was declared. I, like many other young men at that time, thought that it was only a matter of weeks before I would be called up. However this war, different from all others, depended to a great extent on the effort of the engineering industry, and so those of us who were keen to volunteer were politely told that our services in the factory were needed for vital war work.

With an increasing number of women coming into industry, and as the war gradually reaches its momentum, the time is not to far distant when I will be saying, 'Au revoir,' to my workmates. It is an experience which I am sure will broaden my outlook, and I don't expect to get much more out of it! We debase ourselves if we regard our country as a place in which to eat and sleep. History resounds with illustrious names who have given all, yet their sacrifice has resulted in the British Empire, where there is a measure of peace, justice, and freedom for all. But this struggle not only concerns our own land - it embraces the whole world!

Today we are faced with the greatest organized challenge to Christianity and civilization that the world has ever seen, and I count myself lucky and honoured to be the right age to throw my full weight into the scale. We are sent to this world to acquire a personality and a character to take with us that can never be taken away from us. Those who just eat and sleep, prosper and procreate are no better than animals if all their lives they are at peace. The spirit which makes the youth of today volunteer for service in the Armed Forces is reminiscent of the way our fathers answered the call in the last war; I am, of course, remembering the disillusionment they suffered since the start of this war - immense social changes have taken place, and I hope they have come to stay - but I am not forgetting that the most important thing at the moment is to beat the Axis Powers.

Every day when I return home I look for that letter with O.M.H.M.S. on it, which will tell me that I am to take part in the great battle for freedom. It won't be long now!

His call up papers, under the National Service Acts, came through in the spring of 1943, from the Ministry of Labour and National Service Local Office in Waterloo Street, Glasgow; the aforementioned agency said that he was soon to be called up for service in the Armed Forces of the Crown or for Civil Defence.

When George thought about leaving the Mond Nickel Factory at Thornliebank, Glasgow, he thought about some of the disputes in the factory that had taken place, and some of the people involved, but most of all, as he penned his resignation letter to the Transport and General Workers Secretary, he remembered the good times:

Dear Sir, For almost 15 months I have been privileged to be secretary of this branch of the Transport and General Workers Union, but the time has now come when I must give it up.

Casting my mind back to the time when I accepted this job, I remember saying that I would want all the shop stewards to have a say in the running of this branch. I am glad I said that, because take it from me I could never have managed to carry on without the help of the rest of the shop stewards, especially at the start of our term in office.

We have got on not so bad together, I admit we have had disagreements at times, but you get that anywhere, even in parliament.

It is always bad manners to select a few names for special mention, but I cannot help make mention of some of the good work done by the following shop stewards: first of all our chairman, when we started off together we were not great friends, but we both settled our differences and proceeded to co-operate with one another, and I have no hesitation in saying that there is no man in Zenith does more for trade unionism that our chairman. He has been of immense guidance to me and I am sorry to be leaving this job before our term of office is up, because believe me I had no intention of resigning on any other grounds but the present; and I feel I am letting him down, and you also of course, but I trust you will understand.

To Jim Porter and Mary Fulton goes the credit for organizing the Inspection Department where there are only two non-union members. Jim Porter and I used to sit at lunch times and discuss the details of various subjects, and he has also been of great assistance to me. And it is here that I would also like to pay tribute to a lesser-known shop steward who has more or less remained in the

background, but whose opinion has helped me, he is Jonny Russell.
He is one of our back-room boys. His views on a complaint have
often helped me when I was putting it before the management. The
other shop stewards also helped me at different times. And so it is
with a certain amount of regret that I place my resignation before
you.
A greater cause has sounded and I am only too proud to answer it.

George's friend at work Jonny Russell made up a ditty for him
leaving:

> 'He lived up in Busby, a famous wee town,
> A place you all know very well.
> George Walker's the name, a man of great fame,
> Who worked down in Wiggin's Monel.
> Now to the forces, our George, he has gone,
> We all wish him luck, he has plenty of pluck,
> Sure he stayed six years in Wiggin's Monel.
> His mother God Bless her, will miss him so much,
> She will shed many sad tears, I know well.
> It might help her to know, we all miss him so,
> His workmates from Wiggins Monel.
> George was in charge of our Union Branch here,
> And he did his job well.
> He always would fight, till he got what was right,
> For the workers of Wiggin's Monel.
> When the war's over the boys they return,
> Of their famous victory they will tell,
> But we all hope to see George back here,
> As the big cheese of Wiggin's Monel.'

The presentation took place in the works' canteen, 11 April
1943. George had been Branch Secretary since January 1942.
The union responded in the Transport and General Workers

magazine in May, under the heading, Presentation at 7/159 Branch:

'At a social held by the 7/159 Branch in the Zenith works' canteen, a gold wristlet watch was presented to Brother George to mark the members' appreciation of his services during the period he has been secretary of the branch. He has had to give up the position on account of being called up for the Services.'

'Bro. John Sullivan (Area Trade Group Secretary, General Workers' Group), in making the presentation paid a warm tribute to the service rendered by Brother George, his fellow-workers and to trade unionism generally; his devotion to the duties of his office and his work for the welfare of his members, said Bro. Sullivan, had won him the esteem of all.'

'Among the guests at the social were Mr.A.B. Graham (Works Manager) and Mrs Granham. They both wished Brother George every success and a safe return.'

'In reply Brother George thanked the members for the presentation, and said that it would always be cherished as a memory of his loyal friends in 7/159 Branch.'

'Music during the evening was provided by Jimmy Shearer at the piano and Duncan Perry with his accordion. An original composition, sung and played by Jimmy, had everyone laughing. There were no scarcity of singers, and the following workers all sang a song: Miss May Fulton, Miss A. Samson, Mrs J. Wright, Andy Fergus, Aitken Wilson, Stewart Watson, George White, and Charlie Scott. After a very nice tea the floor was cleared for dancing.'

'Bro. Aitken (chairman) desires to thank the management for the use of the canteen and also to the staff for the excellent catering arrangements.'

George's brother Ian, by this time, is with the Military Police, down at Aldershot. At the beginning of the year George from his house at 19 Hawthorn Road once more looks out towards Eaglesham. He stares and wonders. The historic events way out there somewhere beyond the country horizon line, seem to be running away with themselves.

The family, by this time, has settled in at 19 Hawthorn Road, and they like the new house; there is 2 bedrooms upstairs, and downstairs a living room and a kitchen. They have a garden at the back and at the front. To this new address one morning in the spring of 1943, the postman delivers a letter that would change George's life forever.

George, when he first saw the brown coloured envelope lying on the floor just stared at it. Then he picked it up and opened it: 'Would you please report for a medical examination at Dunbarton Road...'

He again looked at the address on the envelope, and the frank mark around the stamp, then he wondered about the department where he had to go to on the other side of the city.

Naturally his mother, Georgina, wondered what would become of her son, but she tried not to think about it. Her 29-year-old son feeling thrilled, told her, "I have to go to Dunbarton Road for a medical to join the army."

This development depressed both parents, for many sons, the same age as George, had been killed by this time; in fact it now seemed part of the daily conversation down at the butcher's shop. The strange expression on someone's face before they said: "Have you heard about..." However, the news of someone being killed could be transferred in other ways too. It was possible to understand an unusual gaze of someone you knew on the street, and sense the tragedy far off: the sad face coming towards you with eyes staring at the death image inside them. It was plain for everyone to see that they had read a tragic letter never to be forgotten. There was a feeling about that the next few years would be decisive in one way or another.

George's father, Johnny, soon picked up, and when speaking

to travellers and workers, who were going in and out of Glasgow, he always mentioned the fact that his eldest son, George, was now on his way to war.

War report: July 1943, British and American forces have landed on the Island of Sicily: a mammoth sea-borne assault. The Germans have put up stiff resistance, but cannot hold the island, and they have retreated to the mainland. The Italians are in trouble. Mussolini has fallen from power. Il Duce's dream of ruling the world is over.

Back in Glasgow, Joe Loss is still on at the Playhouse, and the picture: 'You Were Never Lovelier,' featuring, Fred Astair and Rita Hayworth, is on at the local Toledo.

There were a lot of men being called up at this time, some people said that it was because of all the casualties in Italy and Africa. However, no one, if truth be told, really understood what was going on out there, and the sky, as ever, seemed the best place to interpret the events of the future. In a strange way by the summer of 1943 most people seemed to accept the tread of war as part of life, and the will to win in the young, that strange invisible force, seemed in a terrible rush to get out there and get the job done.

George was passed fit for service, and a few weeks later, 15 July 1943, he got word to report to Brigade of Guards Depot at Caterham near Croydon. This surprised him for he never imagined himself to be good enough, or even tall enough - at just under six feet - for the Guards.

Time passed in the usual way, then one fine morning he made his way to the Central Station in Glasgow: destination the Guards Depot, Caterham. His father went along to see him off. Inside the London train that was packed with soldiers, and civilians, George noticed a tall young man standing opposite him in the compartment. When the train moved off he asked him where he was bound.

The tall young man replied, "I am going to the Guards Depot

at Caterham!" then he introduced himself, "John Allan, from Bridgton," and he shook George's hand.

Meeting a friend made things easier, and soon they met someone else going to the depot; the time on the train quickly passed. The young would-be soldiers, when they got to London, went down into the underground station and made their way to Caterham.

When they arrived at the Depot, George felt terrified; for the sentries were standing to attention like model soldiers, and the picquets in the square were marching with their hands level with their shoulders.

George marveled to himself, "I wonder if that is the way I will soon be marching?"

The building was very old and all the old floors were polished and looked like glass. That night he wrote down on a piece of paper, Diary Of First Few Days:

Arrived at 10.am; a lorry took us from Caterham railway station, then to the Barracks. There are fellows from all over the country arriving at intervals, some for the Scots Guards, some for the Irish Guards, some for the Welsh Guards, Coldstream and Grenadier. First of all we file round a table, where we give a few particulars to N.C.O's. We then are sworn in, two at a time. We go for a bath, and then have to hang around. We get our dinner and are told to wait in a large marquee; our names are called. We then go for our medical and have to wait for some unknown reason in our trousers only - waiting on the M.O. we learn. He arrives, a dapper little man with long side locks and with the rank of captain. After a thorough medical examination we go back to the big cover camouflaged tent. We all get very annoyed and irritated at hanging about so much. The weather is very warm. Aeroplanes are flying overhead all afternoon mostly Spitfires and American Thunderbolts. We think there must be an airdrome near at hand. All you hear is fellows asking: 'Whereabouts do you come from?'

There are lads here many just 18 years of age from all over Scotland. I hang around with two of them that I travelled with: John Allan and Bill Mitchell. We all go for an eyesight test. I past the eyesight test okay. Back to the tent then we get our tea at 5.30. After that we go to the M.1. room, this time for Inoculation and Vaccination. I don't get vaccinated as I was done last year in Glasgow. We go to a store and carry blankets, wooden planks, pillows, to the gymnasium where we are to sleep the night. There must be over 200 of us altogether.

One of the young lads who met George off the bus on a Saturday, when he played football with Eaglesham Amateurs, wrote to him when he was at Caterham in the autumn of 1943:

'Dear George, Please excuse my long delay in writing to you, but to tell you the truth I am not a great hand at writing letters. I did not know that your mother had been in hospital.'

'I hope you are liking army life. Eaglesham is very quiet just now, within the last month about 20 boys have been called up, most of them for the Royal Navy.'

'Mr Proctor (the manager of the late Meadow 11 football team) is running dances in Eaglesham now and again with the help of Mr Edwards, perhaps you will also remember Mr Edwards of the Meadows 11.'

'I hope you will forgive me for not sending the football boots, sooner than I have, but you see I have been always forgetting them.'

'As usual I am still working in the K.P.C.S. Netherlee Branch. I am attending Skerry's College taking a course of book-keeping and also one of Commercial English twice per week.'

'I am still looking for a mouth organ, but I have failed, perhaps if you see one while in England you will bring it home with you.'

'There is no football team in Eaglesham at the present time, but we hope to have one selected by the end of the month.'

'Well, George please let me thank you for asking how my grandmother was keeping, as I think it was very nice and thoughtful of you. I am pleased to say that although she is 80 years of age she can still go to Glasgow and other places all by herself.'

'As it is getting a bit late, I will close my letter hoping that you are in the best of health.'

Your old pal

Stanley

PS: I will be looking forward to seeing your photographs when you get them.

George made many new friends there at Caterham, most of them were younger than he was. The squad received 2 months square bashing: drill parades every day, and lectures on esprit de corps: 'Nemo Me Impune Lacessit'. You only had to look at the place-names on the drum above the Sphinx on top of the word Egypt, when the band passed by you on the parade ground, to sense the history of the regiment: Sevestopol, Flanders, Waterloo, Mons and the Somme. The army number he was given had a certain ring to it: 2701920, he would never forget that.

The trained soldier, McKechnie who came from Mussleburgh, who stayed in their barracks, answered all their questions and tried to help the rookies as best he could.

When the lectures came to an end George was transferred with lots of others to Pirbright. At the camp they received drill and training with weapons: Tommy Guns, Rifles, Bren Guns, Hand grenades, Piats: projectile infantry anti Tank. The Training Sergeant noted as regards recruit 2701920: Nervous, No. Flinches, No. Trigger Pressing, Good. Reliable Man, Yes. Needs Constant Attention, No. Shoots Left Shoulder, No.

Generally Unsteady, No. Careless, No.

Halfway through the training the new recruits are told by the Training Sergeant, in no uncertain terms: "You will not be allowed to walk out of here until everyone in the squad is ready, and has passed the test."

When St. W. Graham's Squad, as they are now known, are ready they get their picture taken: Jenkins, Blench, Mitchell, Burness, Sgt P Howie, Connell, Lawson, Stevenson, Morgan, Clark, Adam, Downie, Fowler, Henderson, Gray, Oliver, Harkins, Allan, Nicholson, Sgt Graham, CSM Hunt, capt Priaulx, Sgt Watson, Tds McKechnie, Lyall, are the names of the men in the photograph - never to be forgotten.

George purchases a copy right away and he hopes one day he will be able to show it to all his friends when the war is over. He gets to know Teddy Blench from Dunfermline, and the Trained Soldier in the squad J McKechnie, from Musslebrough quite well.

War report, 3 September 1943: the Allies have invaded Italy. 8 September 1943 a new Italian government has announced an armistice. Allied troops have landed at Salerno, not all that far from Naples.

At Salerno the Germans in fact nearly pushed them back into the sea; however with the help of a naval bombardment, and air attacks, the Allies managed somehow to get ashore. The Germans, as they retreat up the boot of Italy, construct defensive positions. They will now try and halt the Allied advance and bog down the enemy wherever they can. Whoever holds the high ground in Italy will have a great advantage.

The following month, October 1943, in the rain, the Allies get bogged down along the Volturno River, north of Naples. Then out of the blue, Italy declares war on Germany.

The Germans, right across Italy, have their early defensive positions and fortified lines by this time well in place. And it has come to light that a temporary Winter Line now runs right across the country. This line runs by the rivers Garigliano and Gari, and right in the middle of this line is the town of Monte Cassino.

The local bookshops, in the German occupied area of Cassino, have reported some strange visitors. A few German commanders have popped in to some of the shops to see if they can get any additional information on the formidable surroundings: for they know a huge battle will take place here, and any additional information will be invaluable.

George, one night sitting in the barracks, pens another letter to the Forest Magazine, November 1943:

I have now been in the Guards for over two months and I thought I would write and let you know that I am fit and well. The training here is hard, but I am getting used to it. All our spare time is spent polishing and blancoing, though, of course, being kept busy makes the time pass very quickly. I can hardly realize that it is ten weeks since I left the Fir Copse.

I look forward to the Magazine every month although the September issue was in my locker for almost a week before I had time to read it. I am looking forward to my first leave which will be in about seven week's time - that is, if our squad passes the inspection at the end of the training period. The football season has now started, and I am happy to get a kick of the ball again.

My regards to all at the Fir Copse and to those in the Forces.

The soldiers had trained hard and in December 1943 they got ten days leave, for Christmas and New Year. When George was home he got his picture taken again with his mother and father, and this time with his brother Ian, who was also on leave from the Military Police. Everyone enjoyed themselves as best they could. Then it was back to Pirbright for more training.

13

Wednesday, 5 January 1944: *Fired the Piat (anti-tank) this morning, there is quite a bang from it, and it also kicks a good bit. I received 10- from the Busby Spitfire Fund.*

Thursday, 6 January 1944: *We were all at Alton today. It was a pretty hectic outing. We got our pay tonight, I received £5-5-0. this is Credits Ration allowance, etc.*

Friday, 28 January 1944: *Our squad were taken in an army truck to a moorland away past Puttenham village. We were away all day doing Platoon attacks. I was second in command of the Bren gun section. At night I was told to go and do clerking in the Company office.*

Saturday, 29 January 1944: *I was in the Company office today up till 2pm, then I was playing for 'P' Company against 'O' Company. I was at right back. We won 7-2.*

The next leave is followed by an order to report to Mount Florida school, not far from the famous Hampden Park, Glasgow. George knew the school well; for sure it was at that school he had played the cornet in the Old Boys' Band.

Mrs Adair, whose son had been killed in France, by this time had moved away from Rowallandale, to 248 Clarkston Road, Cathcart. One bright morning in mid-February 1944, she met George's mother, and the two women went along to see George off to war.

When they reached the old school Mrs Adair looked in

through the railings at all the soldiers, and in the middle of the crowd she spotted a familiar face. She shouted, "Look there he is!"

George noticed his mother and Mrs Adair, along with some other women, peering through the railings, and in full battledress he proudly marched over to them.

After George had spoken to his mother, Mrs Adair asked him, "Are you off to war, son?"

George smiled and told her, "Yes, we have to stay here tonight in the school, then in the morning we are off somewhere, but no one has told us where yet."

Then after a pause, he remembered the days when they all stayed together at Rowallendale, Clarkston. He thought about the shops and the people who used to live there. Naturally, he wondered if he would ever see them again. Mother and son stared at each other for a second, then in the strange silence George turned to the woman standing next to his mother and to break the uneasy silence he kindly told her, "You were a good neighbour at Rowallendale, Mrs Adair..."

He chatted to his mother and Mrs Adair, and the time seemed to pass quite quickly. Presently, Mrs Adair looked through the railings again at all the other soldiers in the playground, and she slowly nodded. George smiled at her and thought about her husband the Cartright, and how he used to batter their door at Millerston with his walking stick, for he was stone deaf, and everyone inside would say, "That will be Mr Adair at the door."

Early the next morning Captain Neilson, who had recently come from the Training Battalion's Battle Camp in north Wales, addressed the young soldiers. Word soon got round the men that the young officer's mother had been killed inside the Guards chapel, when the Germans dive-bombed it on Sunday, 18 June 1943. From then on none of the new recruits doubted the commitment of the man who carried a machete down the side of his trousers.

When the young officer stood in front of the young soldiers that morning he told them: "You have reported here today to fight for your country..."

The men listened carefully to what he had to say, then after a few moments the order was given and they marched in threes out of the school. They marched along Battlefield Road, up to the monument where Mary Queen of Scots fought her last battle, down to Shawlands, then over towards the railway station with the funny name, Crossmyloof: something about a cross, a piece of Elm, and a boundary. George in fact used to walk over this way over to Ibrox to watch the football, with his brother Ian, and their neighbour, from Millerston, Joe Britton. Even though it was now an everyday occurrence, young men marching forth to war, many people on the streets stopped and cheered.

As the young soldiers approached the station they could see that an everyday London Midland Scottish train with crimson lake carriages, that usually travelled across the country, sat waiting for them at the station.

Some young soldiers were already standing there on the platform when they got there. The soldiers had arrived from the Deaf and Dumb school at Cathcart. They too had slept nearby last night.

Everyone knew that this ordinary passenger train, sitting at the station, would take them on the first part of an unbelievable journey.

The spring sunshine in some strange way seemed to bring out all the excitement of the time, as it ran along the tracks back to the horizon line. And as the soldiers marched down the steps towards the platform some of them glanced from the bridge through the trees onto the tracks below.

The passenger train, sitting there, made George think about the journeys to and from Clarkston; for this same line ran right past the Mond Nickel Factory where he had worked. The direction of the train, however, puzzled him; for when he thought about it the train could only go back into Central station or out towards the southside. And as he stood there with all the other soldiers on the platform, George wondered to himself, "Maybe the train will take us all the way to London, and then another train, in the morning, will take us to the coast ready for the invasion."

In some strange way all the young soldiers, as they milled about the train station, appeared to be already connected with the momentous events that were happening way out there on mainland Europe. The images seemed to come from ghost writers at the front. The soldiers all knew that this train ride would be no ordinary journey. This journey would take them away from their loved ones. This journey would take them to war. This journey would take them to foreign lands, and for some of them this journey would take them into an early grave.

Although George had been to Pirbright and Aldershot for training, this seemed like a different world. The young officer had still not mentioned where they were going, and a strange silence now seemed to dominate the air before an order was given. An official at the school had instructed them not to speak to anyone. The only thing they knew was that they were going abroad - to war.

George heard a young Guardsman, standing nearby the train, whisper to his mate, "I have heard it's France."

Another said, "No, no, I bet it's Africa."

Then another voice uttered the word, "Japan."

It was natural for the young Guardsmen to wonder, but the wise men among them did not want to think; they just kept themselves busy in some way or other.

Someone shouted at George, "Right you! Let's get these kit bags and packs into the guard's van!"

This suited George right down to the ground, and he went into action at that moment as if enemy planes were about to appear above the peaceful west of Scotland blue sky. After many large kit bags and big packs had been placed in the guard's van, George bumped into a railwayman. The railwayman was on his way up to speak to the driver. George stopped him and introduced himself; after a few polite words had been spoken, he said to him quietly, "Do you know the signal man up at Busby, Mr Calderwood?"

The railwayman's face came alive, as if he had just met a relation, or a friend, of the man just mentioned. He answered robustly, "Yes, I know him, I often chat to him when we stop there."

The railway man understood the order that had been given to him, as regards troop movements, but he also understood that the sons of villagers were important too. He nodded slowly and said, "Should be off soon, son."

He did not say where the train was going and George did not ask him. However, George hoped the railwayman would pass his name on to people who knew him. They stared at each other for a moment or two, then George took another piece of luggage and threw it into the guard's van.

Just before the train left the station, he received another order from the sergeant, "Right, I want you to travel, with three others, in the guard's van and look after the kit bags and packs!"

Not long after this the train left the station and headed away from the city and, after a few miles, instead of going left towards Clarkston - the familiar route for George - it went right after Pollockshaws East towards Kennishead. George looked out of the right-hand window and observed a huge cemetery with black and gray gravestones on the hill. Then he saw the familiar countryside, football parks, and houses he knew so well. It soon became apparent to everyone, who knew the southside of Glasgow, that they were heading down the coast.

Presently, the soldiers arrived at Greenock just before midday and, before the baggage party went to work again to transfer the kit bags and packs from the train onto the pier, everyone seemed to stare at the huge boat sitting at the quay. The soldiers noticed that the boat had an unusual name written on the side of it: The Boissevain. However, the soldiers still did not know where they were going.

A Guardsman speculated at the quayside, as he picked up his bag, "I bet it's the Middle East."

His mate nodded and replied, "Let's hope so, I've always wanted to get a good tan."

When it came his turn George collected his kit bag from the pile, then he followed the rest of the men straight onto the boat. All the soldiers went down below, and there each man was given a hammock.

Soon the ship was full of other soldiers from other countries; the majority of them seemed to be French Canadians. The 100 or so Guardsmen were told that they were to be responsible for the ship, and there was to be no smoking on deck at night, lest the enemy hurled something at them.

When they went up on deck for a look around, a Guardsman, a few years younger than George, turned to him and said, "If you look over there you will see my house at Helensburgh. That's where I stay!" then the young soldier stared at his own house with happy sad eyes. George not long after this met another young Guardsman, Charlie McIntosh, and they chatted to each other.

The boat stayed put in the harbour that day, then the following night, when all the soldiers where tucked up in their hammocks, down below deck, the Boissevain quietly moved off.

The next day the soldiers woke up to find themselves off the coast of Ireland, and the slow chugging movement of the ship made a heavy impression on all their minds.

After they had left Ireland, for a time they had air support; however when they were further out at sea an announcement came over the ship, saying: "There will be no further air support from this point, for we are now too faraway from land," the voice paused, before adding, "however, the Royal Navy will support us." The speaker then lowered his voice, "If this ship is hit by a submarine no other ship will come to its rescue. The orders are that all ships will sail on their own accord towards their destination."

This cheery message made everyone wonder about the evil that lurked beneath the blue green waves and, as the soldiers stared out at sea, many of them remembered articles that they had read about soldiers being lost at sea, frozen to death.

A young soldier, while walking up on deck, turned round and, before stubbing out his Players' cigarette, cracked a joke to his mate, "You think they would tell us where we are going just in case we don't get there."

In the distance sometimes thuds went off like depth charges, but thankfully apart from that nothing much else happened. For some strange reason everywhere you went on the boat during the day there seemed to be the smell of cabbages in the air, and at night all you could hear was the creaking sound of wood.

It soon became apparent that the French Canadians on board did not have the same discipline as the Guards. George noticed that the soldiers spoke to their officers as if they were ordinary soldiers, and the majority of them played cards all day for money, and at night they would smoke on the top deck of the ship.

So the Boissevain sailed on for two or three days in the Atlantic Ocean, and then the ship was joined by a huge convoy from America. Eventually all the ships arrived at Gibraltar, and then the soldiers on board knew they were heading for the Mediterranean: destination either Africa or Italy. Most of the soldiers thought that from now on it would be a smooth voyage, but the strange thing was that this was to be the roughest part of the journey.

When a sailor on board the Boissevain told George all about the sea between Europe and Africa, another illusion in man simply disappeared. The old sea dog said to him in a wise voice, "Guardsman at this time of the year, springtime, the Med is always rough."

One day when George woke up he saw ships moving up and down beside the troop carrier, and when he got up on deck he watched, along with all the other soldiers, the destroyer escorts dart up and down the vast sea. As he watched the ships, someone speculated, "It must be North Africa."

The Boissevain ship, however, sailed by Africa and arrived at Naples, and there an interesting finale took place. A little destroyer, escorting the troopship, dashed up beside her, and all the sailors on board started waving and shouting at all the soldiers on board the troopship.

Standing on deck in the bright sunshine an officer blazed out through a megaphone: "We are now leaving you, our job is finished. We wish you good luck in anything you do in Italy, and we hope it will not be long till you are all home again!"

It was a great sight indeed to see all the sailors cheering, then all of a sudden the little destroyer turned round and headed back along the Tyrrhenian Sea. The soldiers on board the Boissevain now knew for sure that it was Italy they were going to fight. It had taken the ship a week and a half to sail from Glasgow to Italy.

Some of the men on board started talking about how the Allies had landed at Salerno last year, and soon the history of the war in Italy, was discussed by all the soldiers.

Many of the soldiers on board the troopship, before leaving Britain, had read the reports in the press about the amphibious landing at Anzio, 30 miles south of Rome. The landing had taken place on 22 January 1944. Some soldiers on board the ship mentioned that there had been street fighting in San Vittore, until it was taken, and that there had been fighting in

117

the north west of Minturno. Most of the soldiers sailing on the Boissevain ship had not heard of these places. The vast majority understood only that Allied troops, in Italy, had encountered fierce resistance, and instead of chasing the Germans up the country had themselves been pinned down.

The last report that anyone had heard as regards Italy had come from Allied Headquarters, Wednesday, 9 February 1944: 'Advances made by both the British and American troops on the main fifth army front. Fierce fighting continues near Cassino.'

In early February 1944, Monte Cassino was bombed, but the Germans had not been pushed back. Now soldiers from all over the world were here taking part in the conflict: Americans, British, Free French, New Zealanders, Indians, Canadians, Poles, Czechs, Australians, Algerians, Moroccans, Tunisians, Punjabis, Gurkhas, and South Africans.

The question: "How do you co-ordinate men from so many different countries into one fighting force?" is now being asked by all the military men who are involved in the Italian campaign.

14

The soldiers when in action, for security reasons, are told not to keep a diary. George decides that he will keep a mental record of the events that impress themselves upon his senses. When he is out of the line he will record the facts and write them down - who knows one day these recollections may end up in a book.

Friday, 3 March 1944: *Arrived about 11.a.m. at Naples. What a lovely sight, raining.*

The soldiers notice that all along the right hand side of the coastline, opposite the lighthouse, interesting little towns are scattered here and there. They gaze up at Vesuvius. However, as the boat sails into the bay of Naples all the faces on the top deck of the troopship stare over towards the city.

Meanwhile, hospital ships taking the wounded back home pass by the other way. The only normal thing that seems to be happening is that the seagulls are swooping down to meet the turquoise blue sea looking for something to eat.

When the soldiers approach the harbour a small rowing boat suddenly appears from nowhere, and comes close up to the troopship. Two wee boys inside the rowing boat, aged about 10 or 12, shout up to the soldiers for food. A few soldiers throw them some bread, and when they receive the food, the young lads are overjoyed, and they wave back up at the soldiers.

It has taken 10 days for the soldiers to get from dry land to dry land, and as they vacate the boat the rain pours down. In fact the weather is just like it is back home. Presently, they form up on the pier, then after some instructions the young soldiers march off through the city, and for the first time in their lives they witness the total destruction of war. The tragedy hits them full in the face.

The city of Naples has been completely ruined. The people are starving and terrified. Things are in a terrible state. Buildings all around them have been shattered. Ships that have been destroyed are lying on their sides in the harbour. Signs are up everywhere in the city, saying: 'Danger, Cholera, Typhus, VD.'

Last year in September 1943, just before British and American troops landed here on the mainland, Italy unconditionally surrendered to the Allies. Hitler, when this happened, acted quickly and poured more troops in to Italy. The following month, October 1943, however, after some anxious days the city of Naples was taken from the Germans. The Allied troops landed on the beaches in and around the Salerno area. There was fierce resistance, but with air superiority the Allies won the day, and the port was duly taken. In a euphoric mood, with the Germans retreating, some optimistic soldiers, around this time, reckoned that it would be vino and girls all the way to Rome!

The old soldiers in Italy who had fought in Africa said that the retreating German army - even one that knows it cannot win - will try and hold up the Allies wherever it can. And some military strategists on the ground in Italy openly wonder if the Germans have the advantage now: for they know there are many mountains and rivers to be crossed.

Yes, it looks like the Germans, who are now high up in the Apennines, will try and buy time and hope that Hitler's genius will get them out of it. They will resist the British and Allied forces wherever they can.

A fortified line is now drawn right across the country, and right in the middle of this 'Gustuv line' lies Monte Cassino. And on top of a mountain 1700ft high, looking down over the

Liri Valley, known as the gateway to Rome, stands the fortified abbey.

This has always been an important area; the Samnites lived here before the Romans. Monte Cassino became a Roman colony in 309. Mark Anthony at one time had a villa in the town. The abbey was founded by St. Benedict, in the year 529. He built it on top of a pagan temple dedicated to Apollo: maintaining that idleness is the enemy of the soul.

There has been a town at Cassino for 24 centuries where people have lived and sold things. How men built a monastery so high up in the clouds is a wonder in itself. Will the Allies be in Rome in a few weeks? Few military men think so!

Friday, 3 March 1944: *We march through the city, then are driven by army lorries to Rotondi.*

In the pouring rain the new recruits arrive in the afternoon at a small village about 40 miles inland, called Rotondi. This is where the 1st Battalion have their Infantry Reinforcement Training Depot, known to the troops as: I.R.T.D.

At Rotondi, not far south of Pontelandolfo, the hundred or so men in the care of Captain A.S. Neilson are quickly organized into sections, and await further instructions. All the Glasgow lads somehow manage to stay together in the same section, and that night they sleep inside a large bell tent.

On Saturday early in the morning, George opens his eyes and feels uncomfortable. The tent he notices has a hole in it, and during the night rain has come in and soaked him. After F.F.I. (Free From Infection) parade, the soldiers receive their pay of 200 lira.

George after writing home looks around him, and he notices the camp is in a terrible state. There is mud everywhere, and right behind the big tents on top of a hill he sees an old monastery. Inside the camp some soldiers queue up for a cup of tea and a sandwich at the Y.M.C.A. van. Presently, George joins them, and as he stands there in the long queue he notices that you can buy nuts and fruit here.

Some of the lads that night go off into the village of Benevento, situated nearby, and sample the local vino. St Bartholomew's relics were said to have been transported to Benevento. A few of them return drunk. During the night when all is quiet at camp someone in a tent just before falling asleep makes up a rhyme and sings the ditty out loud in a tipsy voice: "I know a girl from Benevento who costs duecento," and his mates laugh.

The second night in sunny Italy the rain comes down again, and the soldiers - the ones with holes in their tents - get soaked once more.

Saturday, 4 March 1944: *My blankets are quite wet.*

On Sunday, thankfully, the rain clears just in time for kit inspection; in fact it turns out quite nice. Some soldiers exchange money, and have something to eat. George thinks the food is not too bad.

The soldiers, on Monday, after receiving their first free issue: 50 cigarettes, 2 boxes of matches, two bars of chocolate, 2 airmail letters, and a green envelope, load their rifles and go off over the hills for training.

Tuesday, 7 March 1944: *Still wet. We buy lots of apples and oranges (1 Lira each).*

Wednesday, 8 March 1944: *Wet again during the night, tent still letting in, mud everywhere. Special parade of Company on Thursday at 3.30.*

George, along with half a dozen Guardsmen, and a sergeant are sent down to Naples in a truck to bring back two Guardsmen. The two men have apparently gone A.W.O.L. They eventually get a hold of them, and on the way back up the road one of the prisoner's spills the beans. He tells George: "We put on American uniforms and set ourselves up in a place called Castellamare. We had a jeep, and I became the Town Major..."

Apparently, they had got away with it, for about a week or so, that is until one day in Naples a man was having a conversation with the Town Major there: "No, I'm all right, for petrol, thanks. I have just made special arrangements with the Town Major at Castellamare."

The Town Major cried out, "What! I am responsible for Castellamare; I give out the petrol in that area!"

The Military Police were of course called, and now this was the two of them heading, back up the road, for a court marshal.

About a week later news comes to the camp that on the Ides of March bombers flattened the town of Monte Cassino, and the monastery. It is a miracle the Germans survived, with so many bombs being dropped on them, but survived they did. In fact some reports say that the tough German Paratroopers are still stationed there.

Other reports say that the German Paratroopers not only survived, but they even pushed the Allies back down the hill. The casualties by all accounts, on all sides, have been terrible. The New Zealanders and the Indians had got the worst of it. More reports follow, and naturally all the soldiers at camp wonder when their turn will come to be sent up the line.

Saturday, 18 March 1944: *Drill parade at Cervinera. I was playing at inside right for the R.I.T.D. against 6th I.R.T.D down past Paolosi. We got beat 2-1. We went in an army lorry. 6 Officers went with us.*

Sunday, 19 March 1944: *Six of us went for a walk to Cervinara.*

The Sunday stroll for the soldiers would have been nice, just like any other I guess, if the war had not been on. Inside the camp George has to do guard duty on some prisoners; these are men who have runaway from the front line, or refused to fight, or have simply misbehaved.

George, on Tuesday, after laying mines, plays football for the Guards against the NCO's (1-7). Later he has a shower, then he walks back to his tent and there he receives his first letter from back home. It is from his sweetheart. The billet-doux cheers him up no end.

The soldiers, the next day, leave the camp at 2pm, and go on a long route march in the direction of Vesuvius. Every soldier has his full pack on, including rations. When they are high up in the mountains the soldiers stare at the unbelievable sight, for Vesuvius is in eruption. George pictures it like balls of flames, like giant oranges heading for the sky.

Pressure must have been building up underground for a very long time, bubbling away just waiting for a route to escape. Was it wrong to understand this world by the events that happen in time and space around us: volcanic eruptions, world wars? Generations pass away and yet whatever it is that makes the earth explode bides its time. The evil in man goes on from generation to generation. But what must it have been like all these years ago on the 24 August 78 A.D. when Pompeii was buried; people choking to death, falling masonry, the air filled with poisonous fumes, thousands killed.

That night the soldiers sleep in a field just outside Gargliani. George does sentry duty between the hours of 7.30 and 9.30, and as he stands there in the dark night outside the camp he feels the cold evening air seep into him, and soon he cannot feel his feet or hands.

Thursday, 23 March 1944, *Reveille at 5.30, after a wash and shave we push on and left Gargliani far behind.*

Not long after this the soldiers are told that they have to go down to Naples and help with the evacuation. They hear that some people have been killed. At Naples they are billeted in a school in the town, not far from Vesuvius. Fortunately for the soldiers, and for the locals, Vesuvius has not got any worse, and eventually only a trickle comes down the mountainside, then the lava stops flowing.

When the soldiers arrive in the area they notice that a lot of people who live beneath the volcano have already managed to come down from the mountainside by themselves. And so after a while the officers, seeing no further risk to the community, decide to send the soldiers and the trucks - that had been standing by to evacuate the people to Naples - back to camp.

George manages to send a report back to his comrades back at the factory just outside Glasgow. The letter is published in the Forest magazine:

I am still feeling fit and well and have more or less settled down in Italy - but I would rather be in Scotland! During our training we had a long route march that took us over the mountains and round Vesuvius, which is a wonderful sight in eruption. I have a little bit of lava as a souvenir. The march lasted for over three days and we had to wear full pack, carry rations and sleep out in the open; at the top of the mountains we had to march through snow. Two pipers accompanied us and we caused a sensation when marching through the villages. We sleep in little tents made fit for only one. It is extremely cold at night. The Italian children have learned enough English to say, "Cigarette for Papa," and, "Hello Jonny! Bread!" The people in the country are very poor indeed and go about in rags.

On Friday the soldiers return to camp and, after a shower, George receives three airmail letters: one from his mother, one from his sweetheart, and one from aunt Agnes at Langholm. His new address is S Coy, 2nd Battalion Coldstream Guards. C.M.F. The Regiment of the Coldstream Guards, he is now with, was first assembled in 1659 at Coldstream in Scotland.

On Saturday all the new soldiers are given a medical, and for some it is really amazing what they find out about themselves; after a blood test George is told he is in blood group O.

Sunday, 26 March 1944: *It was snowing during the night. We all felt very cold. Church service at 10pm.*

Monday, 27 March 1944: *P.T. and lecture, washing in the afternoon. At 3pm we heard our names read out for draft.*

As the soldiers stand in the snow they listen to the names being read out. The surnames of the soldiers make strange sounds; for the voice that shouts the names knows fine well that these are the men destined to fight. All those soldiers detailed to go feel bad because they know it means they will be going up to the front line tomorrow. George's name is among them. He quickly writes some letters home.

The soldiers are given a safe conduct slip of paper written in four different languages, signed by Mark W Clark, Commanding General, 15 Army Group:

'The soldier who carries this safe conduct is using it as a sign of his genuine wish to give himself up. He is to be disarmed, to be well looked after, to receive food and medical attention as required, and to be removed from the danger zone as soon as possible.'

The next day just before getting into the truck, George sends a parcel home containing: cigarettes, sweets, and a piece of volcanic rock from Vesuvius. The trucks leave the camp at 2pm and they travel along the country roads up towards the front line of Cassino.

When they arrive there at 5-45 in the evening, they are shown to their bivouacs. The organization must be good for some letters have already arrived from back home at their new address.

Wednesday, 29 March 1944: *Reveille at 7-15. We were welcomed by the Company. We get plenty of good food and we have been issued with a candle.*

And on Thursday the new recruits are officially welcomed by the C.O. He tells them: "You are now in S Company, 2nd Battalion Coalstream Guards!"

The Second Battalion has been reduced to three companies; for they have lost many men since the beginning of the Italian campaign. The men who have come over with Captain Neilson will now fill this gap. And the letter 'S' will set them apart from the Coalstream Guards. The new company are told that the man in charge of them now is, Major H.D.Cuthbert.

Friday, 31 March 1944: *I wrote to mum and dad. I was on sentry tonight from 9pm till 11pm and then from 5am till 7am.*

George and eight other soldiers from S Company get an unexpected break and they decide to go down to Naples. They get a lift in a T.C.L truck at 8.30am. After a long 3 hour journey they finally arrive in the city around midday, and decide to spend the day there.

Saturday, 1 April 1944: *I had a look around the shops to try and get something for the folks back home, but things are dear. We left Naples at 8pm, just as an air raid started.*

A kind American woman, Mrs Findlay from 729 Manhattan Avenue, Greenpoint, Brooklyn, New York, sent George over a pullover from the States, so on Sunday when all is quiet, he writes back to her thanking her for helping him, and for something to say he tells her about the country area where he was born.

Sunday, 2 April 1944: *I wrote to Mrs Findlay thanking her for the gift of the pullover. Sgt Jones and I made tea in the afternoon. There was no church service.*

At the beginning of the week, even though they are continually told to do different jobs the repetition of camp life makes the soldiers weary.

Monday, 3 April 1944: *We never have a lot of time to ourselves. Got a haircut.*

Tuesday, 4 April 1944, *We had a Battalion Parade at 9.15. The Irish Guards Band played the march past. We had a bath at the mobile baths at Pietato. At 6.30 in the evening the names are read out of those who are going up the line tomorrow. I am one of them. May God help me.*

George, after he hears his name called out, wonders if he will ever see home again.

Wednesday, 5 April 1944: *Always thankful for mum and dad. Left at 1 pm for the front line, we manned trenches during the night. Quite a lot of shell fire, both sides; a man has burned himself.*

Thursday, 6 April 1944: *Slept during the day, took turn at sentry duty. Dug trenches at night.*

George soon gets into the routine of sleeping during the day, and at night taking his turn at sentry duty and digging trenches. Every night a smoke-screen is fired over the town of Monte Cassino to give added cover for the porters going in with food, along the 'Mad Mile'. Some of the soldiers go in and out of the farmhouse nearby.

The platoon sergeant - the man who gives out the letters - arrives, and George gets a wonderful blue airmail letter; it is from his sweetheart.

Good Friday, 7 April 1944: *An old woman brings vino to us. A soldier is taken away to R.A.P. The Naffi stores arrive: Cigs, beer, chocolate, etc.*

That same night George is off duty and he helps the cook. He notices that even though there is continual shelling on both sides the major and the captain seem happy. Thankfully there has been no casualties in his section so far since he has arrived. The positions at the front seem fairly static. Barriers are doing well. He manages to have a wash and a shave, but he feels he could do with a bath.

On Sunday the C.O. manages to come over to where the troops are billeted. He wishes them, "Good Easter!" It may have been Easter Sunday, but the soldiers at the front notice that the fighting has not stopped.

Sunday, 9 April 1944: *Shelling on both sides, some come close to us. It shakes us a bit. The place is infested with rats - it is horrible. A soldier has just shot his finger off; he has been in a bad state since he came here. Same old bully beef and biscuits.*

On Easter Monday the rain and the shells fall. However, the shelling is not so bad at night and so undercover of darkness the soldiers do a little P.T. to keep fit

A trench has been dug behind the farmhouse and it is there they store their empty food cans. When they are inside the stone-building the soldiers watch the rats run along the rafters inside the farmhouse. They know that the rats are trying to get outside at the empty tin cans. Word goes round: "We may go up to the front line - any day now."

In between the shelling a boring routine continues: sleep, breakfast, sentry duty, tea, wash, dig trenches.

George is overjoyed when he receives another airmail letter from his one and only sweetheart. He remembers to write back to his mother and his sweetheart. He tells them that everything is fine, even though the conditions are bad.

The German artillery are high up on the hills and they keep sending shells down one after the other, but thankfully no direct hits yet; some of their soldiers are believed to be housed in steel and concrete bunkers, others are said to be hidden in the rubble of the monastery.

It must be true what they say: for the Germans can see every movement down in the valley and in the plains; nonstop artillery duel, nothing moves without being fired at. No traffic can cross the Rapido river during the day, gunfire 24 hours a day, lights flashing. In this strange atmosphere George notices that the old soldiers pay little heed to the bomb happy sergeant when he shouts at them telling them to get up and out and into the open spaces.

Easter Monday, 10 April 1944: *Still being shelled, but no direct hits. We do a little P.T. in the dark. We are told we may go up to the front line any day now. Shelling not so bad at night. It rains a little; our night off.*

Cassino is a nightmare scene. The smell from the dead bodies is overpowering. Thousands of bombs have been dropped, and the shell-holes are now full of water and corpses; dark angels and dead soldiers from morning to night haunt the place. The smoke screen, fired every night to cover any movement, makes the scene unbelievable. The stone-buildings around the town of Cassino have all now been reduced to rubble.

A strange road exists 'The Mad Mile' where only porters travel up and down to feed the troops. The wounded are brought along this way too when it is possible. It is a two-way road that leads to death. Non stop bombs re-echo in the valley, and the wordless screams of men never seem to disappear from the ears of the living soldiers. When everything does go quiet nothing seems to exist, except the thought of death, bullets, pillboxes, tripwires, booby traps, dugouts, dead mules and barbed wire. Suddenly a fixed line Spandau opens up.

"That will be Spandau Pete again!" a soldier shouts.

Someone jokes: "We should have been conscientious objectors."

"Keep your distance!" yells the sergeant at them.

They say that when the abbey was destroyed the abbot and some the monks walked around the ruins carrying a crucifix, chanting prayers in Latin. And yet in between the shell fire on Wednesday when he is on sentry duty George looks up at the sky and he sees some birds fly by: the blackbird, the mavis, and some sparrows. He often hears them during the night and during the day in between the bombs and the gunfire, and their familiar songs remind him of home. However, when the birds fly away again, George falls back into the nightmare scene of Monte Cassino.

Wednesday, 12 April 1944: *Still getting spasmodic shelling. No direct hits. Lovely day. Rats bad.*

At 10.30 pm on Thursday, in the dead of night, the platoon vacate the farmhouse, and in the dark they quietly make their way into the town of Cassino and up to the front line. Light rain falls. The soldiers have had to put bags over their army boots so as not to make any noise. They are given instructions again: "Don't bunch, don't talk."

It is a nightmare journey through a dark valley of death. When they finally arrive at their destination, somewhere not far from the Continental Hotel, they hide in a brokendown building, and as the bombs fall around them the soldiers make tea.

Thursday, 13 April 1944: *We are housed in a little cellar, 7 of us. We are feeling relieved, soaking wet - expectant.*

George to pass the time counts the money in his pocket. He has got 712 Lire and £2 in English money; unfortunately all the shops are shut at the moment and the money is worthless. Some soldiers use the Lira as bog paper.

Friday, 14 April 1944: *Plenty of corned beef, but not too much water. Nothing much happens. Shrapnel falls from our own barrage. We are given a 24 hour ration box, it is very good. We have bacon, potatoes, cheese and biscuits.*

The Guardsmens bury themselves down in the old cellar and have something to eat as the bombs fall around them: cup discharges from the enemy, and shells from their own side.

Saturday, 15 April 1944: *There are no latrine facilities. We use tins, etc. Most embarrassing and repulsive, the place stinks. Sergeant and I go down to GHQ. All day and all night we have to guard against snipers and fixed line Spanduas. Not allowed out during the day.*

On the first floor of this building they take turns, two hours on, two hours off, to guard their rear against any enemy infiltration. Their opponents, the First Parachute Riffle Division, are known to be tough fighting soldiers. Even though it is dangerous at night a few men take a chance and go outside and move their bowels.

Suddenly one night there was a quick crackle of small arms' fire: Schmeissers firing onto the platoon H.Q. Sergeant Jones shouts to George to go round to platoon commander.

"See if they need our help!"

Although George had an idea where to go, he found it a very dangerous mission indeed. Slowly he crawled in the dark towards the unknown area, and as he moved along through the black night he wondered if he would be lucky and make it. Thankfully he was, for when he reached the spot he came across the platoon commander right away. He was on the phone to the company commander, and the C.O was in no uncertain terms telling him to get outside and organize his men.

Presently, the platoon commander, even though several of his men had been killed, turned to George and said, "No, I think we can cope with it with our own men," and he sent George back out into the dark night towards the cellar.

George had little time to observe the town, however certain images buried themselves deep inside his mind.

Sunday, 16 April 1944: *Cassino town is in ruins, every house is flat. The Officer tells us that he expects Jerry to attack. We get ready; no attack comes. We breathe normal again.*

Monday, 17 April 1944: *We move up into the forward area, this is the front line, not far from the Continental Hotel. We stand on Guard at night with grenades in hand. Sleep during the day.*

The soldiers notice a tank parked in the hallway of the Continental Hotel, just across the road. There seems no end to the conflict as the artillery duels continue all day and all night.

Wednesday, 19 April 1944: *Germans fire on our position and throw up flares. Our 25 pounders silence them, but we had a nerve-racking experience, as the first few shells dropped close to us.*

The Germans to celebrate Hitler's birthday, 20th April 1944, put up a swastika flag somewhere on the hillside. George did not see it but some of the men in the artillery did, and they sent the Fuhrer over a birthday present. Word goes round that their spell will soon be over.

Thursday, 20 April 1944: *We are supposed to be relieved by 7th platoon; they have had casualties on the way up: L/C Healy, Guardsman Robertson; Robertson dies.*

Presently, the section moves back to C.H.Q. and there George and all the other soldiers reflect upon the events.

Friday, 21 April 1944: *We go back to C.H.Q. It is a relief to get away, even if it is only 80 yards back. We have had an easier time. Plenty of tinned meat. Forward platoon attacked by Jerry at 8am, Guardsman Miller is killed, 5 other casualties.*

Major Cuthbert had his headquarters in the crypt at Cassino, and the unusual thing about him was that for most of the time the major stood about in his underpants. Although things got hot and bombs were going off all over the place this humorous expression by the major gave the troops a secure feeling. To George the major seemed a very cool customer indeed.

Saturday, 22 April 1944: *We left Cassino, at 10.30am and got safely back to camp around 4.30am. There we had a welcome drink of tea and a hot spray.*

George's ankle is sore and he tries not to put any undue weight on it. He relaxes at camp by writing another article in to the Forest Magazine:

Just another short despatch to let you know that I am still OK after having been in action. I am now back in camp and feeling none the worse for the experience, although I feel I could do with a holiday after the lack of sleep and discomfort which one experiences in the front line.

I hope people at home are not being to impatient about the progress of the war in this country. If you could only see the mountains and the way the Germans have dug themselves in, you would realize why progress is so slow.

The weather is a lot better now and we have just been issued with summer clothing. I have still to receive a magazine, but hope they are on their way.

Best wishes and kind regards to all the Fir Copse from Italy. (C.M.F. 29.4.44)

Once again the soldiers hear reveille early in the morning at

6.30am, and once again the soldiers have a Breakfast Roll Call. George back at camp tries to recover, but his ankle is still sore. On Tuesday the weather suddenly turns very warm, then it rains on Wednesday. At the end of this momentous month, after drill parade on Saturday, 29 April 1944, the platoon attends a lecture on mines. George is happy to receive that day in the post two newspapers from Aunt Agnes from Langholm. Then on Sunday a church service takes place in the open air with the Welsh Guards.

Monday, 1 May 1944: *On training exercise called 'Spice'. We had to attack a position with the aid of tanks manned by the 7/21 Lancers. It was very hectic. We rode home on the tanks over the fields.*

The soldiers as they wait for action are kept busy. George's section has to do fatigue duties, carrying water, etc.

Thursday, 4 May 1944: *Battalion go up to Cassino again. I was on Company Guard tonight, 8.30-10.30. 5.30-7am.*

On Friday George and three other Guardsmen hitchhike their way to the 2nd General Hospital at Caserta. It takes them quite a while, for they have to get several lifts; but once there George gets his ankle x-rayed, and the fracture is examined by a specialist. Then he heads back to base camp just outside Cassino, using the same method of transport as he came.

On Saturday the weather is very warm, and the soldiers at the camp arrange a game of football for later on in the evening. George, however, does not want to upset his ankle, so he offers to referee the match: Coalstream H.Q. CO. 1 v 0 S Company.

At camp on Monday the soldiers read a letter on the noticeboard from General Alexander, telling them about the forthcoming attack on the Germans.

Tuesday, 9 May 1944: *Had a boiled egg we got from the Italian lad Mario, who had a dog called Lampa. Lt. Sharp killed at Cassino.*

Every night after 9pm at camp George, and a few of the lads

brew up at the Tommy-cookers. The men chat to each other, each man trying to take his mind off the war.

Wednesday, 10 May 1944: *John Weir and George Allan and I get on well together. We always make tea after 9pm on the Tommy-cookers. These two lads are fine genuine lads, who come from Edinburgh and Wishaw.*

Sometimes when the soldiers hear gunfire they look over in the direction of the monastery and sometimes they wonder about the history of the place, and the battles that must have been fought around this area. Indeed, it was not all that faraway from here in 1504 that the Spaniards stood facing the French. The Spaniards crossed the Garigliano at Suio, and the battle started north of Cassino. The Spaniards, after being on the defensive, completely defeated the French.

Suddenly just before midday all hell is let loose, and everyone starts to wonder what is going on.

Thursday, 11 May 1944: *We hear the heavy barrage of guns which are to start an attack by us on the Cassino front. The village clock had just struck 11am when a tremendous barrage opened up; it lasted till 3.30 am. and went on all day on a smaller scale.*

The following night, after tea at the Tommy-cookers, George gets a kip at 10 pm, for rumour has it they will be going back up to the front tomorrow.

The next day Saturday, 13 May, reveille sounds at 6 am, and all the soldiers jump out of their tents. They leave the camp at San Petito at 9.30 in T.C.V. Trucks. Presently, they are taken to a valley near an airfield about halfway up to the front line.

That night George witnesses an astonishing sight. He looks up at the Italian sky and sees for the first time fireflies. He has never seen them before. Some of the soldiers act like little boys and try and catch them; they run around after them as the tiny lights from the fireflies flash in and out.

Reveille sounds at 7am on Sunday, 14 May 1944, and it's a lovely morning. However, there is no church service. The soldiers all go down to the Voltunno River, and there they wash their things in the river. George, when he sees all the naked bodies along the river, cracks a joke to one of his friends: "Looks like a nudist colony!"

Whenever there is time to laugh George laughs, but at night he thinks of home, of his mother and father and brother and his sweetheart, and he prays that he will be spared to return to them.

During the day the soldiers wait for orders, and some of them lie out in the sun, for it is very warm now. A few more days like this and they will all be brown.

Monday, 15 May 1944: *Very warm indeed. Just been told that Dick Hanny, and Capt Fauld, have been killed. Sorry to hear about Dick. He came from St Andrew's. His father was dead and he was the only son. My pals John Weir and George Allan, along with 4 others were detailed to go as reinforcements to the Company. It breaks up the happy home.*

George remembers meeting Dick on the ship the Boissevain and he recollects them standing together on the boat, and someone saying something about a house across from the bay. Tom Fergusson another mate has been wounded; the Germans surprised him early in the morning.

George keeps himself busy, and tries to remember everything that is happening to him, for he knows history is in the making. The film show at camp that night is 'Yank at Eton', but unfortunately an air raid stops the film show after about an hour.

The soldiers, down in the valley, watch as the planes arrive overhead. The B17 bombers bomb the town first then the monastery, and the nightmare scene repeats itself till everything is flattened once again. George has never seen anything like this in his life before - and nobody else has either. What a noise, bomb after bomb, after bomb, after bomb! A magnificent sight!

Tuesday, 16 May 1944: *Reveille sounds at 4.45. Early breakfast,*

136

then packed ready for morning. Battalion moved off to A Echelon.
The mail arrives before we go. It is very warm. We hear the guns of
battle; all around are our Royal Artillery. 6 malaria cases in our
Company at Cassino.

George, the next day, is on guard from 7am to 8 30. and as
usual Captain Neilson reads out the report to the troops of the
latest developments in the battle for Cassino. George around
this time asks many of his friends in S Company to sign the 50
lira Italian note he has got hold of, so that he can keep it as a
souvenir.

The next day some Italians come to the camp and wander
round saying to the soldiers, "Wash?" and some of the soldiers
give them some things to clean. It is noted that they make a
good clean job of the clothes.

Sometimes during the day, or sometimes in the morning, an
ambulance makes its way round into the German quarter of the
town. The troops watch it and are told that the Germans have
received permission to uplift their wounded and their dead, and
bring them back out. Some of the soldiers think that they are
bringing in ammunition, and that the ambulance should be hit,
but no one fires at it. Some of the troops say secret negotiations
are going on somewhere, between secret soldiers.

Suddenly the Poles, who had at one time been held captive in
Russia, make a brave attack up the rocky side of the mountain,
and under a smoke screen they battle over the decomposing
corpses and attack the Germans.

On the other side, from the direction of the Aurunci
Mountains, the Free French start attacking the Germans. The
majority of them are Guoms from North Africa, trained in
mountain warfare. George had heard a few days ago that they
had brought their wives with them, and that they followed the
soldiers around in a caravan.

The next morning a Polish flag appears on top of Monte
Cassino. A poem by Corporal J. Newitt, The Guards Came

Through Again, seems to sum up the euphoric feeling:

The dawn was breaking slowly
With a halo of golden rays
As the Battalion woke up early
For this was the day of days
For today the Wops and Jerries
Were to get a big surprise
And not a pleasant one at all
From the look in those Guardsmen' eyes.

Thursday, 18 May 1944: *Cassino falls. We move in. It is funny to be able to see the place in daylight.*

The strange thing is that some photographers arrive on the scene, trying to capture that all important photograph for the folks back home - some of them are unfortunately blown to pieces by land mines.

Friday, 19 May 1944: *Mopping up.*

Saturday, 20 May 1944: *On the move, we are chasing the fleeing Germans.*

Monday, 22 May 1944: *Night raid, the convoy is attacked; a lot of chandeliers are dropped. Trucks are hit.*

The attack happened late in the evening, after the soldiers had been put into 6-tonner trucks and were heading in the direction of Rome. A German airplane, not all that far along route 6, suddenly appeared and, under the new moon, it dive-bombed the patrol. The plane, as it swooped, strafed the patrol with machine-gun fire, and the soldiers inside the trucks all had to bail out. Not everyone made it though; the Welsh Guards got the worst of it.

The soldiers from S Company, after the Welsh Guards had attended to their casualties, were told to get back into their trucks. However, a few Guardsmen stay behind to watch over the dead.

Further up the road the convoy is instructed to turn right, off the main road; for the Germans are reported to be taking up positions on top of Monte Piccolo and Monte Grande. It looks a certainty that when the dawn comes up another battle will begin.

In fact the birthplace of a famous Medieval philosopher from one of the great Order of Dominicans, St. Thomas Aquinas, is not far from here. The town where he was born is now in ruins.

Thursday, 25 May 1944: *Left for new camp and only stayed one night, it was just outside Aquino.*

Friday, 26 May 1944: *Left for A Echelon at 9.30am; from our new camp we can see the hills where fighting is going on.*

Saturday, 27 May 1944: *I wish I was at Busby just now.*

Sunday, 28 May 1944: *My Brigadier killed, Captain Neilson wounded; heavy casualties. Germans fighting very stubbornly. News comes that casualties in our company are heavy. Another report: 12 are killed, 50 casualties. Very upset at John Weir's death, Hugh Broadly is wounded.*

Many of the lads from A Echelon are rounded up and sent up to the front line right away, for it is serious. They must hold the line. George's name is called out, then for some reason recalled. The soldiers all hurry away up to the front.

Monday, 29 May 1944: *The Company clerk goes up the line and leaves me with his papers, etc. I am on sentry duty tonight, 12-3am. One enemy plane comes over during the night.*

Tuesday, 30 May 1944: *We move up today to Mt. Pillico. The Brigade comes out of the line. I don't feel too well. I have diarrhoea and feel very weak. The atmosphere in the camp is different with so many lads missing. I visit their graves.*

George finds the graves of his fallen comrades, by looking for the number 270 on the wooden crosses. The men are buried here and there all over the place, some where they have fallen.

Later on that day, as they are making their way along the road towards the German position, George starts to feel unwell. He

139

does not know what is wrong with him, his head is light, and he has a fever. He is always having to drop his trousers.

George fights on; however he doesn't get any better and later on he has to stop and say to the platoon sergeant, "I don't know if I can carry on, sergeant."

The platoon sergeant looked at him and said quickly, "Well, make your way back to the nearest First Aid Post, we can't send anyone with you."

Even though fighting is still going on all around him, George walks back down the road, hardly caring about the gunfire. Halfway along the road he meets the company clerk. He is rushing up to the battle - things have got so bad that they have sent for the penpushers. Just behind the company clerk, George sees the storeman with his gun in his hand. George feels like lying down, but he keeps on going; and somehow later on that day he arrives at the Forward Aid Post.

In the back of an American ambulance at the Forward Aid Post is a raving man. He is ranting away as mad as a hatter. George slumps down beside him, and mutters to the First Aid man, "What's wrong with him?"

"Malaria," replies the orderly, as he looks up at the new arrival.

Presently, the American ambulance man takes the casualties to M.D.S and George is laid down there inside one of the big marquee tents. A medical orderly comes over and takes a blood sample from his finger. Then a little later a doctor appears on the scene and looks at a blood slide. In a knowing voice, the doctor says to George, "Guardsman, have you ever had malaria before?"

"No, sir."

The doctor gazes at the soldier, then he adds in a professional manner, "Well, I'm afraid, you have got it now."

This news was a shock to his system, for George thought he would end up like the madman he had met inside the ambulance at the Field Aid Post. He had always taken his

Mepacrin tablets - one with his dinner every day - even though some of the soldiers said that the tablets made you impotent.

The doctor, pleased to hear that he had taken his Mepacrin tablets, explained, "There are three types of malaria, you understand, and you will be pleased to know, Guardsman, that you have contracted the lesser of the three."

He left the 132nd Field Ambulance the next day at 4.30pm for the 18 C.C.S. and once there he receives Quinnie. He sees some terrible sights in the ward, but the spirit of the British fighting soldier keeps him buoyant.

Friday, 2 June 1944: *We get some laughs in the ward.*

A nurse hands him a fly swatter: "To keep away the mosquitoes," she says with a smile.

George by the end of the week begins to get his appetite back and his temperature goes back to normal, although he still feels weak especially in his legs and back.

Sunday, 4 June 1944: *Feeling a bit better. Had a table jelly for tea. 2 C.P.M.s came in today with malaria.*

George, to pass the time, writes to the Greenbank Church magazine, The Good Neighbour, telling them that he is none the worse for his experiences, and that he carries his Services' edition of the Bible with him wherever he goes. Then he pens another letter to the Forest magazine:

I am in hospital with malaria, I was taken ill at the front and was brought down the line in an American Field Ambulance. Fortunately, it is of the mild type (due of course, to the tablets we have been taking every day). I am now having Quinine three times a day. We are quite comfortable here - it's quite a change to sleep in a real bed after dugouts and slit trenches. I was taken ill at rather an unfortunate time as we weren't very far from Rome then. Goodness knows where the Battalion will be by the time I get better.

We are now allowed to say that we were in Cassino when it fell;

the Germans pulled out as they were being surrounded. What a terrible state the town is in - it is so bad that I cannot think how they will ever rebuild it.

In the February issue of the magazine I noticed two photographs of two Welsh Guardsmen and I saw that they were wearing the Divisional sign as I am, so I hunted around for them. Gdsmn Deer of Ash Grove, I understand, is still in North Africa. Gdsmn Morgan has been in Cassino with us but was left there when we moved up the line. Still I shall probably catch up with him before long. I have also tried to trace the whereabouts of Tommy Begbie. I am sorry to learn that he has been wounded and I hope it isn't too serious.

Remember me to all the Fir Copse especially to those in the Scrap Store. And so I will end this dispatch from sunny, but much battered, Italy.

P.S. If the 2,000 ton Press is extruding sausages, tell them to send some over here! (5.6.44)

Tuesday, 6 June 1944: *Feeling very well, only my legs are a bit week.*

Wednesday, 7 June 1944: *Transferred today to No. 9 convalescent camp. 8 of us in a tent.*

George, lying there in his bed, listens to the radio, suddenly the music stops and an announcement comes over the airwaves: "Under the command of General Eisenhower, Allied Forces have begun landing on the northern coast of France..."

A great cheer immediately goes up all over the camp and all the soldiers rejoice. This event they hope and pray will bring about a quick end to the war.

Friday, 9 June 1944: *I am excused PT.*

Saturday, 10 June 1944: *L/C Feilding and I went to Capua to an Ensa show: Stars in Battle Dress. Then we had tea in the naffi and a tin of cherries.*

After the Church of England service on Sunday, L/cpl Fielding and George go down to Naples. They get a lift in an army jeep. It's a lovely run. At Naples they notice that the Canadians there have a mobile cinema and first class canteen facilities.

George and two MP's, on Monday, go to Capua to see a show, but unfortunately the show has been cancelled.

Thursday, 15 June 1944: *Our tent was duty tent today. We had to dish out the meals. I am now on daily Mepacrin.*

Friday, 16 June 1944: *The depot is right on Highway 6 which runs through Cassino to Rome. There are a lot of Italians on the road, some making for Rome others coming from it.*

Monday, 19 June 1944: *I went over to our B Echelon at Piemonte and collected all my kit and equipment; I met corporal Fisher, he told me that CMS McDade had been killed.*

Tuesday, 20 June 1944: *Went to Capua I bought a mirror and a bottle of scent, for back home.*

Wednesday, 21 June 1944: *Taffy Trooper and I hitchhiked our way to Naples; review this morning by the Major. He says that I may have to go back for a medical.*

Thursday, 22 June 1944: *Most of the depot have moved up towards Rome; we that are left are having a fairly easy time of it.*

Friday, 23 June 1944: *I went on a day trip to Naples from the Convalescent Depot. I paid Charlie Prentice a visit at the 65th General Hospital in Naples, I then went to collect my photos in via Roma and wrote some letters back home from the Royal Palace.*

Monday, 26 June 1944: *Went to Riardo a walk, and visited the old castle on the hill. We had cherries and apples on the way back in the jeep; terrific thunderstorm tonight never saw anything like it.*

Wednesday, 28 June 1944: *We (those left as a rear party) went up and joined the Battalion Depot which is 5 miles from Rome. We then travelled up Route 7 through the Fontine marches which were flooded. A lot of German guns and machines were lying about.*

Friday, 30 June 1944: *I Saw the MO today, and I have to carry on with exercises; received a letter and £2 from Henry Wiggin's*

Comforts Fund.

At the start of July 1944, the weather was very warm, almost unbearable, and sometimes George would go up to the farmhouse for a drink of cold milk. After being up for a review, he sent a parcel home: scent, cigs, tobacco, a fountain pen, soap and a Jerry belt.

Friday, 7 July, 1944: *Left Depot at 10.30am for No. C.R.U. (at Terni). We passed through Rome, arrived in camp at 3.30.*

It was on this journey that George met corporal Freddie Adams, and they became friends. He was from Ayr. The two of them have to wait for further instructions at Rotondi.

After about ten days word comes through that they have to be part of a detachment, sent up to join the 1st Battalion Scots Guards at Terni.

On the train, just before they move off, they are joined in the compartment by another soldier, an English man. The strange thing was that when the train stopped in the middle of nowhere, an hour or two later just north of Rome, the stranger stretched himself, and muttered, "I'm getting out here for a piss." For some reason George felt he would not return, and when the train moved off again, Freddie and George looked out of the window for the English man, but he had vanished leaving only his Great Coat behind him in the train.

Saturday, 8 July 1944: *Another batch of Guards arrive, 'Ginger' Morgan is among them. We talk of old times and of the old lads of the original squad who have lost their lives.*

At Terni, north of Rome, George joined the 1st Battalion of the Scots Guards. The 1st Battalion had not long broken out of Anzio. George was put into Left Flank. He was told that he was now finished with S Company.

When he hears about a religious service George takes communion in the field. The padre has a word with him after it, and when he finds out that George is interested in learning Italian the padre gets hold of a book for him so that he can study the language. The first Italian George learnt was: "Non abbiamo niente! I tedeschi ci hanno portato via tutto!" for everywhere they went this is what the peasants said to them.

Sunday, 9 July 1944: *Didn't feel too well this morning. Wrote to mother and father, 'Taffy' left to join the Battalion; raining.*

Tuesday, 11 July 1944: *Left C.R.M. for Transit Centre on South African Petrol Wagons; meet Indians at Staging Post.*

Wednesday 12 July 1944: *Left transit Camp at 1pm, by T.E.V.D. for unit. Went back to A Echelon which is just beside Lake Trasimene.*

Sunday, 16 July 1944: *We hear that Captain Neilson has been killed by a mine. C.S.M. Brown also killed and Sergeant Jones too.*

Monday, 17 July 1944: *I had a good day with the New Zealanders who are in the next field. They have a small barrel of vino, also a guitar, so we have a sing-song. They are fine lads; a corporal of the Coldstream's and I were invited for a late supper with them. We had toast with butter and honey; got to bed at 11.30.*

In war things happen so quickly and it is sometimes hard to keep up with the pace of events; one night George is sleeping in a farmhouse then the next in a field at Cortona, then the next night he finds himself somewhere else. In Arezzo he looks at a photograph on the mantelpiece in an empty house. The photograph is of a young mother, about his own age, and her three lovely young daughters. Inside another vacated house he picks up identity cards and membership cards and reads them: P.N.F. Anno Era Fascista 21349. Gioventv' Italiana Del Littorio X1X P.N.F. Nel nome di Dio e dell'Italia giuro di eseguire gli ordini del DUCE e di servire con tutte le mie forze e se e necessario col mio sangue la causa della Rivoluzione Fascista, and wonders why this has all come about.

Friday, 21 July 1944: *Left the farmhouse at Cortona for Arezzo. It was dark when we got to our new billets - which is a lovely big house. I have a sofa for a bed.*

145

George and a few other soldiers, at the beginning of August, leave Lake Trasimene by plane for Naples.

Wednesday, 2 August 1944: *Air evacuation, I enjoyed the trip of 1 hr 45 mins, Red Cross very kind, arrived at 92 General Hospital.*

Saturday, 9 September 1944: *Went to Naples this morning with Corporal Fergusson spent most of the time in the palace NAAFI, I bought 2 boxes of almonds and posted them off back home. They cost 5- each.*

Sunday, 10 September 1944: *Police duties from 6am till 10am; at 4pm Corporal Booth and I went to the Italians house for dinner; they gave us spaghetti etc, very nice people.*

Sunday, 24 September 1944: *On guard duty tonight on prisoners compound. About 9pm, three prisoners escaped, two were caught in the morning; we are all up before the R.S.M. to give an explanation.*

Back home at the beginning of November 1944, another letter arrives from George and is published in the Forest Magazine:

I am now with the Ist Battalion Scots Guards and I am still fit and well but, as usual longing to get back home. During these last few days I have had quite a few experiences, but I want to tell you about one example of the atrocities the Germans are carrying out. Years ago I never believed all the stories I read about the horrible crimes the Germans were capable of doing but I have now seen some with my own eyes. As you will know from the newspapers and radio the Allied Armies out here are fighting in the mountains just before Bologna. In our advance a few days ago we came across two separate lots of men and women and children lying dead just outside their farmhouses on the hillside. There were 36 in all and they all had been shot by SS troops as a reprisal against the activities of the Partisans in this part of Italy. It was a horrible sight; we all agreed that it was the worst we had seen and were unanimous in our opinion that any nation who does this cannot hope to win. Actually, the Partisans have helped us quite a lot out here, and we have retained some with us for the time being as, with their knowledge of the countryside, they are very helpful. Italian Alpine troops also help us by assisting with the mule teams which bring the rations, ammunition, etc, up the mountains.

I am now with a new Division; one advantage is that when we are out of the line we get plenty of sweet tea or coffee from the refreshment vans.

Please remember me to all my friends at Fir Copse. I hope it won't be long till I see them again. Best wishes and kindest regards. (C.M.F. 1,11,44)

Around this time George receives an unexpected airmail letter from America. After staring at the strange writing and marks on the envelope, he opens it and reads it:

May 27   *729 Manhattan Avenue*
1944   *Brooklyn 22*
                                   New York

Hello George,
You will never know how surprised and pleased I was to receive your very welcome letter, I have knitted dozens of pullovers, helmets & scarfs, and to think that the one and only answer I got was from you, a fellow Scotsman. I was born and brought up on Garscube Road near Partick Thistle's park, I guess you know where that is all right, of course that was many years ago, so you will see we are not so far apart, and little things like these make the world seem smaller. Many happy Saturday afternoons I spent in your home town of Busby. It was a favourite picnic place for us, and just to hear the name brings back many happy memories. I have plenty of relatives in this terrible business, even nephews and nieces on both sides, any more than that I am not allowed to say. We meet quite a few Scots over here both army and navy, and get to know pretty much how things are over there. Well, George, I think it is really

wonderful of you to spend time out of your all to brief rest period to
thank me for the little I have done, when you and your buddies are
doing such a whale of a job over there, and I only hope it won't be
long till we are all enjoying a peaceful life again. Good night
George, and God be with you.
Yours sincerely
Mrs Findlay

Wednesday, 10 January, 1945: *Heavy snow.*

Saturday, 13 Jan 1945: *Leave to Florence, from the "Casa Di Horror."*

Friday, 2 February, 1945: *Advance Party.*

Monday, 5 February, 1945: *McGregor got word his mother had died.*

Wednesday, 7 February, 1945: *I am now a Lance Corporal. Leave for the line tonight, relieve the Indians.*

Thursday, 8 February, 1945: Fairly quite. It rains and snows and we are rather uncomfortable.

In the winter of 1944/5, George found himself on guard inside a large house in the Argenta Gap. The house had been bombed many times. One night while sitting looking out of the window an officer came over and spoke to him. The Officer said, "I am not happy with the corporal we have; I would like you to take over as lance corporal of this platoon. The next time we are out of the line I will get you up in front of Major Tuke."

George, thinking of others, replied, "There are a lot of old soldiers in the platoon, sir, would that be all right?"

The officer reassured him, "Yes, I have spoken to them, it's fine."

After this George went down into the basement of the house. He had not long taken up his position and was looking outside again over the door when all of a sudden two shots were fired by a sniper into the house. The shots went right through the door. George and another Guardsman quickly moved away.

148

The house was obviously under surveillance, and from that moment the soldiers inside the large house understood that they could not go outside until it was dark.

Another time when they were concealing their position somewhere near the front line, they were paid a visit by a very famous regimental man. George had first set eyes on this man about two years ago in the guard room back at Pirbright; George and 5 other new recruits, at Christmas time, were sent to clean up the dining room. When they arrived at the dining room suddenly a regimental voice cried out, "Guardsmen!"

All the new recruits thought they were in for it, for not walking smartly, or being behind time.

The regimental man, who had shouted at them, looked at the young recruits, then he added in a barrack square voice, "Would you like a drink of beer?"

This was the voice of the famous Freddie Archer; and he was standing beside a big barrel of beer. Freddie Archer had served in the First World War, and he wore putties just like you did then. He had won the military medal. The regiment meant everything to him.

George had heard, like everyone else, that when Freddie and his wife were out walking with the pram and they came across an officer, he would give his wife: "Eyes right!" and when an officer telephoned him, he would salute him on the phone. There were many wonderful stories about him.

In the winter of 1944/5 Freddie Archer had decided to take his week's holiday at the front and spend it with the troops. This night when the soldiers were in a dangerous area, Freddie Archer crawled into their dark cellar where they were positioned. And when the regimental sergeant major came across the Scots Guards he crouched down beside them, sniffed the air twice, and because the enemy was near, he said in a low dramatic voice, "I smell REAL soldiers!"

This was the greatest compliment he could have paid to them, and it cheered them up no end. George like all the other soldiers thought the world of him.

The most regimental man in the British army had a terrific sense of humour. One time when he was out walking with his batman, they came across some pigs in a pen at R.I.T.D. Rodondi. The regimental sergeant major turned to his batman and exclaimed, "Look at these pigs lying there - they're like big dirty Grenadiers!"

War is a horrible thing from start to finish and for some it brings out the worst in their character. That winter George came across a village somewhere in the Argenta Gap. The whole of the village had been out sheltering in a field. When the danger had passed a man from the village brought his daughter over to a building in the town, near to the dormitory where the soldiers were staying. There were lots of soldiers from everywhere in this area. He locked her inside a house there and, before heading back for his wife, he asked George in a worried voice, "Will she be all right?"

George assured him, "Yes."

Two soldiers, passing by at this point, saw what was happening and, when the man was gone, one of them suggested: "Right let's just burst down the door and..."

George stopped them and reading the situation, he said: "No you won't," and the corporal threatened to tell the officer. "I won't allow you to do that - she's just a young girl. I've given my word."

"Oh, don't worry..."

George, just to put them right, told them about a lecture given by the commanding officer that he had heard recently: "If I ever hear of anyone raping, I will be very severe on them," he said.

On a lighter note he also remembered what the medical officer had said to them that day, when lecturing them on V.D. "You put your penis where I wouldn't put my walking stick."

In the Apennine Mountains in the winter of 1944/5 the

weather was very cold - so severe in fact that they rushed out the first issue of new string vests to the troops. The soldiers were also given a bar of Cadbury's milk chocolate with raisins every day to fortify them against the cold. Other regiments from other countries fortified themselves against the cold as well.

One time when an Indian Brigade was being pushed back by the Germans, George's section was sent in to help them. The situation thankfully got better after reinforcements had arrived.

Later on that day, when George was digging a trench, two Indian soldiers came past him. One Indian soldier was carrying a pail of cha and the other a big plate of chapattis, and just when they were passing by him a heavy stonk of German mortar fire came over.

George signalled to them to come over and into his trench; for the bombs were like tramcars crashing to the ground all around them. The Indians hurried over and presently jumped down inside his trench, and they all crouched down together. The 'horrors' were just something you had to deal with in wartime - the chapattis didn't half smell good, though.

The Indians were still trembling when the attack finished, but they wanted to get the food up to their men, and after a few moments when there was a lull in the fighting they went on their way.

It was very cold up in the hills in the Apennines, so much so that the soldiers could only last for two or three days up there, then they were brought back down again.

George, one-time up on the hills, found it interesting to watch the artillery duels. After watching the enemy fire onto a farmhouse, opposite him, he reckoned it took them seven or eight goes before they hit their target. They would pepper it, go round about it, then they would hit it.

He did not know the name of the area he was in, but because of the continuous German mortar fire they had been tied down here for a while. After another heavy stonk that seemed to last forever, the soldiers popped their heads up, and sometimes the patter could be quite good in the trenches: "I bet that Jerry has got a castle on the Rhine," someone hollered.

After a long bout of shellfire George shouted back, "Are you all right over there!"

Someone else cried, "Are you there, John?" but no word came back from the other trench.

Unfortunately, the men not far away in the trench had received a direct hit. Two or three mortars had come quite near to the other trenches, but they had just been lucky. When comrades were killed some of the soldiers expressed the view: "Well, I guess if your name's on the chitty, that's it. There is nothing you can do about it." However, the optimists in the trenches took a different view: "A shell never falls on the same place twice," they said, and were happy at that.

All the way up through Italy the platoon had to stop at canals and bridges: for many had been destroyed by the Germans. One evening when they could not get any further on, for this canal was quite deep and broad, the Commander in Chief radioed for help. The Royal Engineers were sent up by HQ to make a preparatory bridge. This they did and when the temporary bridge had been successfully accomplished all the soldiers stood back and watched the first tank roll over it. Unfortunately, the driver of the first tank misjudged the bridge and it toppled over into the river. An officer up in the turret managed to jump out, but the other three inside the tank could not get out.

George could hardly believe it and in complete horror he turned away from the sad sight. After a few horrifying seconds had passed, he turned to the officer standing beside him, and said, "Is there nothing we can do, sir?"

The officer murmured something to himself, then he replied, "No, Guardsman, they will be dead by this time - it is impossible to get out of a tank once it is underwater."

Delaying tactics were adopted by the Germans in the Florence area. They positioned Spandues in haystacks and when the Allies came upon them, the Germans would open up and try and pin down the advancing troops. Sometimes the soldiers had to wait for a tank to come up, before the Germans would scatter.

One time when 8 Guardsmen, were moving up the road suddenly a machine gun opened up on them. The soldiers all jumped down into the side of the banking, along the dry river bed, and as they lay there all they could hear was the ratatat-tat of the German machine guns as they fired at them.

Thankfully a South African tank was not far away and fired at the three haystacks and set them alight. In fact if truth be told the old heads in the South African division set fire to everything that was in their way, as they made their way up Italy.

An Italian man, up a little further, appeared outside the gates of an expensive looking mansion house. He watched the South African tank for a time, and when the soldiers approached him, he shouted at them in an anxious voice, "You can't come in here with that!"

A South African soldier on top of the tank told him bluntly, "If you don't open the gates we will blast them open!"

One dark winter's night in the Apennine Mountains in an area called Castiglione dei Pepoli, George, a corporal now, was in charge of a mule escort. The escort consisted of three Guardsmen taking six mules loaded with cans of water and food up to the troops on the hillside. So with George at the front of the food patrol they set off, hoping that everything would be all right.

Suddenly out of the black night, not far along the road, the head of a Coldstream Guardsman popped up from one of the trenches and, as George passed by him, the joker whispered to him in a comic voice, "Okay, Jock!"

Apparently, the Coldstream Guards had sentries in the trenches all along the pathway. When they got to the shack, where the soldiers were staying, the escort party quickly unloaded the water off the mules; for they wanted to get out of this dangerous area as quick as possible.

While the mules were being unloaded the Coldstream Guardsmen gave the porters back the empty cans. The empty cans had a piece of metal attached to the cap, and a chain that dropped down inside the can to keep the caps from getting lost.

Now on the way back down the cans started to rattle and the mules started to trot, and while this was going on the Jerries were putting Very lights up, and firing mortars. The Germans seemed to know the time when the food went up. And with all the lights and mortars flashing it became quite scary.

The mules sensing that something was up started to trot even faster, wanting to get back down the hill to their usual place. Needless to say, with so much firing going on, the porters all scampered back down the hillside along with the mules.

One morning while George was up in this area he received a letter with an unusual heading on it:

SUBJECT soccer trials
Main HQ Eighth Army CMF
Tele Ext 73, M 9004 A.23 Feb 45:
2701920 Gdsm

1   The above-mentioned soldier has been selected to participate in the Eight Army Soccer Trial at CESENA stadium on 7 Mar 45.

2   This trial match is one of a series which it is intended to hold with a view to selecting the best Eight Army X1. It is requested that this application should be given every consideration.

3   Personnel should report to A Branch, Main HQ not later that 1300 hrs and should bring their own football boots (if in possession) towel, soap, and eating utensils.

4 In order that reliefs can be arranged where necessary it is requested that you signal this to HQ as soon as possible stating if the above-mentioned can be made available.

What wonderful news! George was being pulled out of the line to play football - he didn't have get some stick, from his mates, though.

Another letter arrived this time from his mother; she told him that Tommy Murphy had been killed in Italy. George, as he read the letter, thought about how they had played football together at Busby and Eaglesham, and how they used to meet every Thursday night to organize the team up at Tommy's house. Stanley Smith had also been killed at the Normandy landings; George could hardly believe Stanley was old enough to be a soldier, he was just a boy when he carried his boots down to the pavilion for him - how sad, poor Stanley.

Those wonderful days seemed so faraway now, playing football up at Eaglesham, getting off the bus and meeting the local lads like Jock Weir and Wullie Melville before the game. George's dad knew that the news would affect him, and to cheer him up he popped a card in with the letter that had a poem on it from the well-known southside bard, Corn Crake:

> *This part of Busby where we live*
> *Amongst the working classes,*
> *We haven't very much to give*
> *Our local lads and lassies*
> *As poor as Nazareth you know*
> *Yet pleased and thankful too,*
> *Perhaps this trifle serves to show*
> *We still remember you.*

Jock Bennet from Aberdeen, sometimes in the middle of the night in the trenches, just had to have a fag to steady the old nerves, but there was absolutely no way he could light up in the dark; for the Jerries would spot the flame and just throw something at him. Black soldiers out on reconnaissance smoking cigarettes described in the novel by Remarque, All Quiet On The Western Front, had a real ring to it now. George and a few others, who knew the signs, would gather round, then one of them would put a Great Coat over their heads. Jock would get under it and thankfully after a couple of puffs everything would be fine.

Monday, 26 March 1945: *On guard from 4pm till reveille.*

Tuesday, 27 March: *Playing for the battalion team today against the London Irish riffles. We won 1-0. I got a kick in the right shin and knee.*

Monday, 2 April 1945: *Communion in the field.*

One day Corporal Freddie Adams and George were told to go with a major from the Royal Artillery to a big house over looking Porta Garibaldi. Once there the major set up his position at the window, and looked through his silver periscope in the direction of the canal.

After the information had been relayed back down the line, shells were fired towards the German positions. Unfortunately, the Germans soon understood what was going on and they dispatched their own shells towards the big house overlooking the port.

Things got very hot indeed and after about six or seven shots were fired the major turned to the two guardsmen inside the big house over looking Porta Garibaldi, and he said diplomatically, "I think we'd better get out of here, chaps; I think they have got our range."

George and Freddie, both on the ground floor at this point, were pleased to hear him say this, and presently everyone jumped out of the back window of the big house.

Now the Germans, like the British, had at one time been in

this house and had used it as an observation post. In fact the Germans had used the ground, below the window, as a latrine - literally sticking their bums out of the window. Well, Freddie jumped right into the latrine, and as they ran for their lives they all started to laugh.

L/Cpl 2701920
Left Flank
1st. Bn. Scots Guards
14th April 1945

My Dear Mother and Father,
It seems a long time since I last wrote to you, but I just haven't had the time, as we were busy. I am now a bit further north, and we are just waiting on word to go up further.
I have been getting your letters regularly and I got father's letter with the Good Neighbour in 5 days, all letters up to 2gms come by air now.
I am glad you are both keeping well, I too am quite well, I am sitting at the side of my little tent which the sergeant and I share. It is very warm here, I hear we are not to get K.D. this summer, they probably think it will be over soon.
We have a new platoon officer, he is not long over here, he is very nice, his name is Mr Simon Bland, and he is quite young.
I was awfully sorry to hear that Uncle John has been wounded, according to what you say it looks as if he has been wounded by shrapnel from a big shell. It is a bad place to be wounded, and I do hope he survives. It was very good of the authorities allowing aunt Jean to fly over.
I am glad you are receiving my postal orders, I am going to see the Company Clerk and see if he can get me some more postal orders, I have written a little note and if we leave in a hurry he will get them and post it for me. We are just sitting waiting on the word, 'Go!' I hope Will R. Rose makes a good job of the films with Ian in

them. Many thanks for your letters father with the Good Neighbours. I know you are always thinking of me, we will have a good time when I get home, mother can make a dumpling. It shouldn't be very long now till it is over, the armies in Germany are getting nearer Berlin, and you will have noticed that the armies in Italy are now on the move. We get tremendous support from the air force these days, they absolutely rule the air out here. In our last position up the coast we watched the R.A.F. Spitfires drop bombs on a little town called Porto Garibaldi, we had a front seat view, one pilot had a bit of misfortune his bombs didn't release properly, they exploded in the air and damaged his plane, and he bailed out and landed on some marshy ground which the Germans held, but he succeeded in contacting a patrol from 'B' Company so he is all right. At this moment there have been about 50 German prisoners marched along the road to the POW cages, they are all shapes and sizes, not all the enemy troops out here are Germans, some Czechs, Lithuanians, and all sorts, these ones give themselves up more easily.

It is very warm out here just now and we will soon get sunburned if it keeps like this.

A year ago I had my first glimpse of the front line that was in the much bombed town of Cassino, we went into town about midnight and relieved the New Zealanders, the Germans kept putting up flares and the ruined town looked a terrible sight in the light of these flares.

Please tell all the people who might be interested that I am fit and well, I don't get much chance to write being a corporal I help the sergeant as much as I can.

I know that you will be worrying again, and it is only natural that you should, but I shall continue to take as much care as possible. I wasn't going to tell you, but we are on the move again, but it is best you should know.

It is a great pity president Roosevelt has died he was a great man, I was a great admirer of him, and I loved to hear him speak on the radio; in my humble opinion he was a better man than Churchill *or Stalin. Remember me to Ian when next you write. It looks as if he is going to win the bet, good luck to him and all the lads of the B.L.A. they are doing well, all my love and best wishes, have patience and I will write again as soon as I can, till then I say cheerio and good luck. It shouldn't be long now. Your ever loving and devoted son George XXXXX God bless you both.*

In the spring they found themselves in the Po Valley. This night the soldiers were searching for some of their own men; reports said that the Germans were retreating. The commander wanted to reach the River Po by nightfall, although he called it by another name: "The Jolly Old Piss Pot."

They walked on till they came to a canal, but the bridge was broken, so the soldiers stopped there for a rest. However, the tanks supporting the soldiers could not get across it, so the soldiers were sent on ahead. They advanced on a bit and just when it was getting dark they came across a farmhouse. George slowly opened the large door of the outhouse, and in the dark he heard the sounds of bleating sheep inside. He closed it quietly. Not long after this the soldiers settled down near the farm and awaited further instructions.

In the dead of night, when everybody was getting tired, shots were suddenly fired at them from the farmhouse, across the way. The Scots Guards opened up with all they had and some men were killed on both sides. There was no doubt about it the Germans were inside the building opposite the outhouse across the courtyard. It looked as if the Germans were going to try and hold back their advance.

The major thought about advancing and presently he gave an order for George's section to get ready to move: for his section was next in line. A German tank could be heard moving about behind the farm. Someone said that it was retreating.

George by this time had his section in a gully by the side of the road; however he felt that the Germans were regrouping behind the farm and that the tank was slowly getting into position. As a precautionary note, as they waited for word, George told his men to take their shovels and picks out of their packs.

Major Tuke went into one of the farmhouse buildings to set up a command post, and not long after this the German tank suddenly fired a shot right into the farmhouse, and there were some casualties.

The battle started and realizing the situation nine or ten Guardsmen outside the farm had to retreat back a little. The Guards fought bravely and as they ran passed the farmhouse the Germans started firing from all sides.

As the battled commenced Joe Calder, from George's platoon, somehow managed to get on the other side of the canal. In the dead of night he shouted over to George that he had been wounded.

George shouted back over to him, "Are you all right, Joe! Do you want me to swim over?"

Joe said that he was all right, and somehow got back to the other side of the canal. When they got back to the broken down bridge, where they had advanced from, George could see that Joe had been shot in the arm - the man from Barfield Road, Buckie in Banffshire had been lucky.

However, Major Tuke and the rest of the men, who had survived inside the farmhouse, were not so lucky, for they were captured by the Germans and sent up to Austria to a prison camp.

Monday, 23 April, 1945: *Ran into Germans just passed Mollinello. lucky to escape; 3 killed, 14 taken prisoner.*
Wednesday, 25 April, 1945: *Bologna.*

L/Corp 2701920
Left Flank
1st Bn. Scots Guards
C.M.F 25th April 1945

My Dear Mother and Father,
I have been very busy, we have been kept on the move, and it has been almost impossible to settle down to write.
I am happy to say that I am all right, although I will confess I am very tired, however the main thing is I am safe and sound, after a very narrow escape the night before last. We were advancing along the road leading to the Po River, we were clearing houses and had taken some prisoners when all of a sudden the Germans fired on us from a farmhouse. We all took cover in a ditch and got organized.
I have been in charge of the section for a week now as Sergeant Henderson was hit by shrapnel on the leg and is now in hospital, but he isn't seriously wounded. Well, I am not going to tell you all that happened that night: how only my Bren-gunner was wounded on the arm. There were 2 killed and 14 taken prisoner so you can imagine it was a near thing. Our Company Commander was taken prisoner. His name was Major Tuke, and I am sorry to report that lieutenant Winter, the officer who was my platoon commander, was killed yesterday, he was Training Officer at the R.I.T.D. and was only up in the line one day when he was shot.
I took two prisoners on Sunday morning, they came at daybreak, I got a pocket watch from each of them and 800 lire (£2). I gave one of the watches to Jock Bennet a fellow in my section who comes from Aberdeen. There are a lot of prisoners being taken out here, quite a lot are Russian soldiers giving themselves up, they all say they had to fight for the Germans, because they got very little food in the P.O.W. camp. I am writing this on the banks of the Po, goodness knows where we go from here, we are staying in a house, and I have just been told that we are to be here all night so we will all get a good night's sleep. I have been getting your letters, and

today I received one from Aunt Agnes, she tells me John Dick is a little better and is now in England. I hope you have heard from Ian, he will be going through the same experiences as I am: very little sleep, in a different place every few hours, digging trenches, sometimes three in a night. I am glad you received my P.O.S. I will send you some more whenever I get the chance.

We get a lot of eggs these days, you see when we are advancing there are no civvies to be seen they all go into big dugouts away in the middle of a field, and they put a big stick with a white flag on it. So you will have an idea what happens, a lot of looting takes place.

Well folks this war shouldn't last much longer, so keep being brave and I will certainly look after myself. Cheerio for now, I send all my love and best wishes and will write again as soon as possible. Your ever loving and devoted son God Bless you, George. XXXXXX

The Germans could not get all their horses across the Po at Cortona, and they left some behind to fend for themselves.

George one afternoon a few weeks later came across a big workhorse in a field. The poor thing had been hit by a shell; it had a terrible wound in its hip. There and then he decided to get his Tommy gun out and shoot it. George, before he killed it, led it over towards a big shell hole, so that the horse would fall into it when dead.

A funny thing happened for just when he shot it a woman from the local village came running out, shouting in Italian: "Wait a minute, till I tell my husband!"

Not long after this a few more people appeared, with big knives and plates, and presently they started to cut strips of the horse's hindquarters. Then they took the food back with them to the village.

George mentioned this incident when he wrote his next letter back home, but he didn't want to say who it was that killed the horse:

L/Cpl
2701920
Left Flank
1st Bn Scots Guards
27 April 1945.

We are still having a bit of a rest, so I am going to write down as much as I can, because when we get on the move again we don't have much time.

I'm still safe and sound, but I confess I am feeling very tired, we all are - but I will be all right in a few days.

The sergeant hasn't come back yet, so I'm still in charge of the section.

This is a good house we are in, we have mattresses down on the floor for beds, so we have a good soft bed. The people are very kind, the woman of the house is a spinster, there is only her and her father and her brother. She is 52 years of age, but like you she doesn't look her age, and she is working morning till night.

There are scores of horses running about the country wild, they are German horses, but were left behind, just before they retreated across the Po. The Germans use a lot of horse-drawn transport, proof of the fact that they must be short of petrol. One of the horses had been wounded it had a shrapnel wound on its body. The lady of the house and her brother asked me if they would be allowed to chop a piece off for food for themselves. I said yes they could have it all, so the Italian men got a hold of an axe and some big knives and they cut pieces from its hind leg. They say it makes good butcher meet and they wanted me to taste a bit today, after it had been cooked. I told them that we Britishers would be very hungry before we ate a horse.

There are an awful lot of dead horses lying around the roads here, they have been shot by the R.A.F. and by the big guns of the Royal Artillery. This morning they rounded up all the Fascists in the town (Cologna) and made them bury all the dead horses. We haven't

163

crossed the Po yet, we done all the advance up to it so there are others carrying on now, but it wasn't very difficult to cross the Po, the Germans seem to be disorganized over here.

I am glad to hear that Jock Higgins is home, he must have had an awful time, I am always inclined to be sentimental, but I have my mind made up not to be sorry for the Germans, and when I am in action I always say to myself, these people killed Donald Adair, Tommy Murphy, George Thompson, Stanley Smith, etc, therefore I will not be sorry for them, and in the last action when 20 of our company were killed and 14 taken prisoner, I fired quite a lot with my Tommy Gun, and if I killed any Germans I am not sorry for them. Please tell Jock Higgins I was asking for him, I got your letter 29th yesterday, it was the one written on ordinary paper in a white envelope, it came in 5 days. I smiled when I read your remark to Ian about me always writing wither I was busy or not, I just thought I have let you down, because the letter I wrote yesterday was the first for a good few days, but really the last ten days have been terrible days, on the move here and there, patrolling, digging trenches, no sleep, clearing villages, seeing awful sights, and all that goes with war, and that last fight we had crowned the lot.

Sorry to hear about the fellow McFarlane, is that who George Bell is Batman to?

I was speaking to Jim Hogg yesterday. You will soon be at bowling again father that should help to take your mind off the war for a little while.

I have a photograph of a prisoner I took, I will send it in the next green envelope.

We had rain last night, the first for weeks. It was kind of you giving Mrs Adair a hand to clean the house, I am sure she appreciates it. No please don't send any parcels, we get plenty of food. I had a letter from Henry Wiggins & Co, telling me that they will give me a job after I get released, and they want me to let them know if I had any special training since I joined the army. I will probably reply saying Yes: leading men in action. Cheerio for now *keep being brave. It won't be long now, love and best wishes your loving and devoted son, George. XXXXXX*

Sunday, 29 April, 1945: *Left Bologna this morning, crossed the Po, stopped at canal.*
Wednesday, *2 May 1945: Left canal this afternoon.*

15

Thankfully the war in Europe was over by the time they had reached Venice, and the soldiers were given a day off to visit the city. Venice for the soldiers had many interesting facts, not least la Serenissma had not been conquered until taken by Napoleon in 1797. George got his picture taken in Piazza St. Marco along with his mates.

For a time they strolled around the strange city like tourists, sometimes looking over at the 14th century Doge's Palace, or at Sansovino's Library of St. Mark's, built a century later. Everyone was overjoyed. They could hardly believe it was all over.

It was not long, however, till a rumour went round the men that they were to be sent home for a holiday, then posted out to the East to fight the Japanese.

USA General, Mark Clark, sent everyone a letter, dated May 1945, with the heading: To the Soldiers Of The 15th Army Group:

'With a full and grateful heart I hail and congratulate you in this hour of complete victory over the German enemy, and join with you in thanks to Almighty God.'

'Yours has been a long, hard fight - the longest in this war of any Allied troops fighting on the Continent of Europe. You men of the Fifth and Eight Armies have brought that fight to a

166

successful conclusion by recent brilliant offensive operations which shattered the German forces opposing you. Their surrender was the inevitable course left to them, they had nothing more to fight with in Italy.'

'You have demonstrated something new and remarkable in the annals of organized warfare: You have shown that a huge fighting force composed of units from many different countries with diverse languages and customs, inspired, as you always have been with a devotion to the cause of freedom, can become an effective and harmonious fighting team.'

'This teamwork which has carried us to victory has included in full measure the supporting arms which have worked with us throughout the campaign. The services that have supplied us have overcome unbelievable obstacles and have kept us constantly armed, equipped, and fed. The magnificent support which we have always had from the Allied air and naval forces in this theatre has written a new page in the history of cooperative combat action.'

'Our exultation in this moment is blended with sorrow as we pay tribute to the heroic Allied soldiers who have fallen in battle in order that this victory might be achieved. The entire world will forever honour their memory.'

'The war is not over. The German military machine has been completely crushed by the splendid campaigns waged by you and your colleagues of the Western and Russian fronts. There remains the all important task of inflicting a similar complete defeat on our remaining enemy - Japan. Each one of us in the 15th Army Group must continue without pause to give the full measure of effort to that task wherever we may be called upon to serve.'

'I am intensely proud of you all and of the honour which I have had of commanding such invincible troops. My thanks go to each of you for your capable aggressive and loyal service which has produced this great victory.'

'Men of the 15th Army Group, I know you will face the task ahead of you with the same magnificent, generous and indomitable spirit you have shown in this long campaign. Forward to Victory. God bless you all.'

The Germans who by this time, 29 April 1945, had retreated to the top of Italy had signed surrender terms at the Royal Palace Caserta. Not faraway the residents of the unsettled city of Trieste on a cloudy day rose up. It had been reported that the German garrison at Trieste had surrendered when they understood it was not the Yugoslavs soldiers they were laying down their arms to.

The Yugoslavs wanted to control all of Venezia which included the main cities: Trieste, Pola, Gorizia, and Fiume. The Italians, who had the overwhelming majority of the people in the region, wanted the British and Americans to protect them. The First Battalion the Scots Guards were sent in to keep the peace.

On the way there the Scots Guards, Left Flank, stopped at a farmhouse somewhere on the outskirts of Trieste. They found, just by the farmhouse, there was a lime pit. There the Guards painted all their web equipment with white lime so as not to look like fighting soldiers. It was a good idea for them to look like military policemen. The powers that be did not want them to arrive in Trieste looking ready for a battle.

The soldiers as soon as their belts and gaiters had been whitened all jumped back on board the New Zealand tanks, and advanced along the coastal road towards the troubled city. A New Zealand division had taken Trieste and had accepted the surrender from the Germans.

Saturday, 5 May, 1945: left Camponogaro at 7 arrived at a place about 15 miles from Trieste at 1pm. Kit whitened.

The First Battalion Scots Guards had been chosen by the authorities to 'show the flag' for the British. Most of the soldiers

168

that were sent in to keep the peace knew that the Yugoslavs laid claim to Trieste and the Italians wanted it back. The Yugoslavs had the Russians on their side.

However, it was well-known in the West that the Triestini people were against communism; in fact some people in the city longed for the old days of the Austro-Hungarian Empire to return. Reports in some of the newspapers said that it would all be sorted out at some peace conference; many people believed that this would be Trieste's greatest test.

Just before the soldiers entered the city they came across Radio Trieste, and after some consultation a guard was put on the Radio station. Then after this they made their way further into the town.

When they arrived in the city there were a few partisans marching around, putting flags up, and shouting Sloveve slogans. Then big buxom women appeared, as if from another world. The women stood guard on every street corner, and as more partisans arrived in the city panic set in.

The partisans played havoc with the locals: stealing women's coats, and taking cars off anyone who dared to take them out onto the streets. The partisans painted the walls with red paint. Needless to say their dour attitude, and their revolutionary slogans did not make them attractive. Some of the citizens ran up to the Scots Guards shouting for help, but George knew that the soldiers could do little to assist them.

Sunday 6 May, 1945: Church service, arrived in Trieste, tense atmosphere.

Later on that day the Yugoslav army arrived in Trieste from Pola. However, by this time the Allies had their tanks in the town and had taken up positions in different areas. Thankfully they soon got things under control, and the people of Trieste turned to the Allies for help.

Monday 7 May, 1945: On guard at 55 area.

The victory parade took place down at the seafront and the unusual thing about this march past was that the soldiers had to march with live ammo, just in case of trouble erupting. Thankfully the parade passed peacefully. Everyone in Trieste came out that day and watched the march past; it was such a lovely day too with all the boats in the harbour. A few days before the victory parade took place the Company Sergeant Major, J. Horsborough, came to Sergeant Jiggy and said, "Sergeant, I would like you to organize a victory celebration for the men. We have booked a big hall in the Stazione Marittima down at the seafront."

Sergeant Jiggy, as he walked down towards the Stazione Marittima to organize the night out for the troops, noticed a Class 4 ship, the Orion, in the harbour. And lo and behold not long after this he bumped into a sailor, John Nicol, who came from his home town of Busby. There were around 300,000 people living in the city of Trieste at this time, and here he bumps into someone he knows. Back home John had stayed just down the road from him. The world is like a small village right enough: 'Il Mondo e` piccolo pease,' as the Italians would say.

Sergeant Jiggy greeted him warmly and invited him to the night out that they were planning. Then the sergeant took him to the mess where John was given a good meal. Likewise John responded and invited the newly promoted sergeant onto the cruiser the Orion and there on board the ship Sergeant Jiggy tasted white bread for the first time for many years.

John gave him plenty of shag for the soldiers back at the barracks. When leaving the ship, so as not to draw any attention to the tins in his pockets, Sergeant Jiggy gave a smart salute as he left the Orion ship, and the sailors on board did not stop him.

So many people turned up on the night of the dance that they had to close the doors. Sergeant Jiggy had invited a lot of young

Sgt W. Graham's Squad, Catherham 1943.

In the Barracks at (Caserta Muti) Trieste 1945.

*With Indian soldiers
and Italian children.
Naples, June 1944.*

*Bill Keith and George, with three
Yugoslav girls.*

*L/sgt Brown L/sgt T Morrison,
George, L/sgt D Allan, on the Main
road to Fiume from Trieste.*

*George with, Yugoslav officers,
and Itailians, and Lt Morrison,
handing over French. Line, 16
Sept 1947.*

No. 21 Road Post, George with L/cpl Cordingley.

Football Final Prizegiving,
(George centre) at Trieste 1946.

Road post Duty at Pola, with Lupo, and a local lad.

With George Bell, Trieste, 19 May 1945.

The soldiers rejoice in Venice, war in Europe is over.

Geoge with John Nicol, from Busby. June 1945.

V-E Day Trieste.

At Spittal, Austria.

Jiggy with Sergeant Keith, Rome 1947.

Freddy Adams, and George, at Palmanuova Station,
coming home, Nov 1947.

Some personel of Left Flank at Lipiza, summer 1946.

ladies along for the soldiers, and of course the young ladies told their friends. It was a very successful night indeed, and everyone enjoyed the food and the dancing. The band played old and new numbers, and all the young ladies from Trieste took something home with them, like a sandwich, or a scone, or a piece of cake; for food was still in short supply at this time in Trieste. Sergeant Jiggy, even though it was the end of the war, still thought it funny to see young women slip food into their bags.

Two pipers from the Guards played at the end of the night and a photographer took a picture of the wonderful scene. There was only one flash point during the night, and when it happened the Guardsman on the door quickly sent for Sergeant Jiggy, "Come down quick, serge, for some sailors are trying to push their way in!"

When Sergeant Jiggy got to the front door he noticed that there were indeed a lot of sailors outside. Sergeant Jiggy could understand them wanting to get in, but he told them: "If you continue to take this attitude I will send for the Street Patrol - and they will soon sort things out!" and the sailors, although disappointed, slowly moved away.

Saturday, 12 May 1945: Company had a dance. Met John Nicol who is in the navy. Slav soldier found shot.

Sunday, 13 May 1945: Visited John Nicol aboard the Orion. Church service with rifles.

A few days later Company Sergeant Major Horseborogh, who was in charge of events, sent Sergeant Jiggy a letter complimenting him on his organizational skills: "I would like to express my feelings, by thanking you very much for your most energetic work at the bar. I am sure you will agree with me that our job was well done."

Friday, 25 May, 1945: Won South African food parcel. Monday Company went down to the beach for the afternoon. I felt sick coming back, went to the r.a.p

Tuesday, 29 May, 1945: Felt much better today, I think I got too much sun yesterday.

Wednesday, 30 May 1945: left C.R.S today at 3pm. Thunderstorm tonight.

Saturday 2 June 1945: Corporal Lawson received the American Bronze Star.

Thursday 7 June 1945: Wrote to John Warren, on Guard tonight.

Sunday 10 June 1945: Church in the morning. Walked to Procecco with Sgt Kelly.

Friday 15 June 1945: Cricket today v "S" Coy. We lost by over 140 runs. Received £2 from Wiggins.

In the early days the soldiers were not allowed to walk out alone, there always had to be at least three or four of them just in case things flared up. George found it very interesting, and for a time he watched the Yugoslav soldiers march along the streets with their captured German arms. He thought they were mainly country folk. He noticed how on every street corner three or four partisans would gather and stand there. The partisans, as they stood guard, chatted to each other; in fact the partisans washed and shaved just by the side of the road.

The Italians in Trieste did not get on with the Yugoslavs at all. Sometimes the Italians would point at the Yugoslavs, and cry to the Scottish soldiers, "Cento anni addietro!" meaning that the Slavs were a hundred years behind the times.

George, one morning, found a dead Yugoslav soldier not all that far from the Guard"s lookout post in the middle of the town. The man had been murdered during the night. The war in Europe may have been over, but George knew that this would remain a dangerous city, till the map of Europe was redrawn.

The First Battalion the Scots Guards made their presence felt, and after a few weeks things thankfully settled down and the incidents lessened. On V-E Night the sky over Trieste lit up and nothing, not even fanaticism that came from self-determination, or rumours about a clandestine Yugoslav state already in existence, could dull the joyful noise of peace over war.

Sometimes the soldiers played football in the main square, and one day while playing for the Battalion Sergeant Wullie Henderson lost his balance and twisted his ankle.

Left Flank
1st Bn. Scots Guards
C.M.F.
17th June 1945

First of all I must apologize for putting the wrong date on my last letter, I dated it the 17th where it should have been the 14th.

I received your letter this morning when I came back from the church service.

The service was conducted by the Rev. R.Selby Wright (The Radio Padre) and was a very good service indeed. He is now a chaplain to the forces, and is at present attached to an Indian division who are quite near us. When I say an Indian Division you will be wondering why he is attached to an Indian Division, but to tell you the truth there are a good number of British soldiers in it, the majority of course are Indian, but there is one Brigade of British Infantry and all the artillery will be British, so are the Royal Engineers. Our Padre invited him to come. At the end of the service, he said he remembered taking the service at the Guards Depot and you will remember I was at it.

Our Company Commander has just told us this morning that we will have to stick this lonely spot for another month, then he thinks we will move in to Trieste for the winter. We all hope he is right.

The first batch have left our Battalion for the month"s home leave, and another five go on Tuesday. A Battalion has about 1000 men so you will see how long it will take to come round to me, of course once they start taking us home by plane the scheme will operate more quickly. But, I repeat, I am quite happy and content here, this life is all right.

We got the photographs today they are quite good, although the sun was too strong and a lot of lads have their faces screwed up. I will try and post one of each off to you to night.

It was nice of Willie Shaw paying you a visit, I am glad he liked my letter, I just thought I would send it to show him that he was not forgotten about. I know when we used to be having a rough time a lot of us used to say, people will never know what we are going through and if they do they will soon forget. I used to say that my parents would always be thinking about me and that was the main thing.

I hope you don"t find Alf and Uncle Jimmy too much bother. Away in the distance it looks as if it is going to be wet tonight, so I will get all the stuff in the tent. I have the tent to myself as Sergeant Kelly is away to Florence for a week"s leave. My other Sergeant is in hospital, he broke his ankle playing football. Cheerio for now and good luck, you loving and devoted son. George. XXXXXX

Not long after they had arrived back to Trieste the senior officer spoke to George, and he was duly promoted to sergeant. When a man becomes a sergeant in the army he is invariably called something other than his title by the other soldiers. George for some reason was called Sergeant Jiggy - something to do with his surname, and a character from the First World War, or so they said.

Well right away Sergeant Jiggy decided on two things. Number 1: he would always respect the soldier and call him by his rank: "Guardsman MacDonald report to HQ, you are needed down there," and number 2, he would make sure that his writing on the noticeboard would be in clear bold print, so that everyone would understand their duties.

Sergeant Jiggy, one day while out walking in Trieste, met a Mr Scherian. This man had a butcher"s shop in town. Mr Scherian stayed in the Piazza Antonio Rosmini and, after getting to know Sergeant Jiggy, he offered him a room for nothing, near to where the soldiers were staying. Sergeant Jiggy took the room, for it was not all that far away from where the soldiers were billeted in the middle of the town.

Saturday, 7 July, 1945: Left camp for a ten day tour of the countryside north of Goriga, arrived at Podresca.

Tuesday , 10 July, 1945: Left for Savogna.

Friday, 13 July, 1945: Big Festa in Savogna, dancing and drinking.

Monday, 16 July, 1945: Recce over Caporetto.

Tuedsay, 17 July, 1945: Arrived back in camp from our stay in the Caporetto area.

Thursday, 26 July, 1945: *We moved into Barracks in Trieste.*

For a time some of the soldiers were sent into the country and billeted at Lippizzano, north of Trieste. The famous Spanish horses had been brought here in 1580. The stables were quiet when Sergeant Jiggy arrived, and the paddock was empty. The Germans, when they retreated from Yugoslavia, had taken all the horses with them. The Guards had put up tents in the paddock area, and army tradesmen had started to build wooden huts for the soldiers inside the grounds. A large number of German prisoners were used as labourers for this exercise.

In the local area a great big house, not all that far away from the paddock, was used by the head the communist party. Apparently a few soldiers, who had been out celebrating the night before, had hauled down the triumphal arches in front of the house. Word went round the camp that the Yugoslavs were furious and the commanding officer was going to have to apologize to them; in fact some of the soldiers were instructed to put the triumphal arches back up again.

Wednesday, 8 August, 1945: Company V.E. Day Celebrations.

Thursday, 16 August, 1945: I am now a paid L/Cpl.

One day when they had returned to camp after a march along

the country roads with the colours, the R.S.M. noticed that the German prisoners had stopped work on the roofs of the huts, and were watching the parade. The R.S.M. raced over to some of them and instructed them to salute the colours. Sergeant Jiggy, as he marched along, glimpsed out of the corner of his eye the R.S.M. climb up a ladder and confront some of the German prisoners, "Salute the colours!" he shouted at them.

During the Second World War the Yugoslavs had used the old Austro-Hungarian barracks; unfortunately they had kept their mules in the basement, and the place was full of dung. Local labour was sent for (boys and men), and they soon cleaned it up. The First Battalion Scots Guards, when everything was ready, moved into the barracks, along with the Second Battalion Coldstream Guards, in all about 2000 men.

As time passed it soon became clear to everyone that the Yugoslavs wanted Trieste for themselves. Field Marshall Alexander, because of the situation, left a small detachment there. Thankfully, with the soldiers now in the city, the people of Trieste all came out and walked around the shops, and slowly life got back to normal. And as the fate of the city was still to be decided the Yugoslavs also left a presence there, but many of them drifted away back to the countryside.

Peacetime duties and drill parades commenced to the sound of the pipes once again. Sergeant Jiggy seeing a new face about the place introduced himself to Piper Penman. The young man had just come out to Italy and the sergeant quickly showed him the ropes.

Trieste could be a very cold place indeed, and when the hurricane wind the Bora blew along the Adriatic it raged at a terrible speed. The soldiers were told that it could blow people of their feet: "Vento forte." Sergeant Jiggy noticed ropes attached here and there around the city. Some people said that the ropes were tied here and there to help people stay upright when the hurricane raged.

In the middle of Trieste in a big square called the Piazza dell"Unita`, the Governor"s palace was quickly transformed into an information centre. And every day outside the palace people queued all day, every day, for news regarding loved ones, lost in Russia, or in other parts of Europe.

One day Sergeant Jiggy standing guard outside Navy house, on the left hand side of the square, got his photograph taken with Guardsman George Bell who came from Eastbourne. Then a day or two later, when he was once again in charge of the guard outside Navy House, he glanced quickly over at the Municipal Building, built by Giuseppe Bruni. Sergeant Jiggy wondered about this quarter. He knew bands played here in the summer. The beer he had been told was cheap: sixpence a glass. After this he watched the people of Trieste walk about, then he stared back over at the Governor"s palace directly opposite him.

This day for some reason was to be different from others; just around lunchtime in the middle of the square an Italian man came out of the crowd and came right up to Sergeant Jiggy.

The Italian man said in broken English, "A man out there in the crowd wants to give himself up, but he doesn"t want to give himself up to the Yugoslavs."

Right away Sergeant Jiggy told him, "Tell him to walk straight up the steps and in here, and I will be waiting for him just inside the doorway."

The Italian man went back out into the crowd and presently an ordinary man carrying a small suitcase walked towards the Loyds Triestini building, up the steps and then inside the door.

Sergeant Jiggy greeted him with a friendly, "Hello!" then he said to him, "You"re safe at last."

Inside the Loyds Triestini building he was made at home, someone even got a cup of tea for him. The man declared in a happy German-English voice, "I come from Danzig, I have been in the German navy, in a submarine, but I escaped, and I have been staying here in Trieste with a family for weeks. I have

177

never been out - only now when the Allies are here, did I feel safe to go out."

The man looked around him and even though now he was safe inside the building, he seemed to feel the clutches of the partisans as if they were not all that faraway. The man from Danzig felt that the partisans, if they had got a hold of him, would have killed him without asking too many questions.

The man from the German navy then sat down inside the shipping office and waited for the soldiers to arrive. He knew he would be soon transferred to a prisoner of war camp, and hopefully after that back home. Before the soldiers arrived to take him away to HQ, the man from Danzig turned to Sergeant Jiggy and said, "I want to give you my submarine badge as a token of my thanks and friendship," and as he handed it to him, he shook the sergeant"s hand.

The 1st Battalion planned to troop the colour in Trieste in December 1946. And the soldiers practised and practised, till everything was perfect. The Regimental Big Band was sent for from London; however, two days before the troop the bora began, and the parade had to be cancelled. The people of Trieste were disappointed, for they were so looking forward to it.

One day a new recruit joined Left Flank in Trieste. He was a German Alsatian dog. He had been handed over to a British officer, by a German Officer after the German officer had been taken prisoner. The Alsatian dog liked his Scottish friends and Sergeant Jiggy looked after him. The soldiers called the dog Lupo, the Italian name for wolf, and the dog seemed to take to it.

Well, Lupo was a wonderful dog in many ways. The soldiers swore that he could read the blue name of the "Scots Guards" on their epaulettes, for when any strangers appeared in the barracks, like Royal Engineers, or Royal Army Service Corp, or the Artillery, Lupo would bark at them.

Another dog, Prince, a fierce Alsatian, became well-known too around the barracks at this time. One night two Guardsmen went down into the town with Prince and visited a cafe bar. Unfortunately, the soldiers had too much wine and they fell asleep where they sat.

When it came to closing time the waiter could not get anywhere near them to waken them up, for every time he tried to rouse them Prince growled at him. The owner of the cafe got in touch with the Military Police, but when they got there they couldn"t get near the soldiers either.

Someone telephoned the barracks, and about 2 o"clock in the morning two Guardsmen went down to the cafe bar to see what was going on; thankfully Prince recognized them, and the two Guardsmen roused the tipsy soldiers and then they all went back up to the barracks.

Around this time Sergeant Jiggy, along with a corporal and ten Guardsmen, had to take two three-tonner trucks down to an ammunition dump somewhere near Venice. They were instructed to load the ammunition onto some trucks: grenades, piets, and rounds for rifles and Tommy guns - apparently there was to be a big training programme soon.

However, when they reached the outskirts of the city they ran into a Yugoslav demonstration, and the demonstrators started shouting at the soldiers in the three-tonner trucks. Sergeant Jiggy thought it wise to make a detour round them. He knew the streets well around this area and he told the driver where to go, thus avoiding the hotheads in the parade.

The R.S.M had been worried and when they got back to the barracks he asked the sergeant what he had been up to, "Where have you been Jiggy?"

One day at a road post somewhere in the mountains two men from a farm came up to speak to Sergeant Jiggy and asked him if he could take one of their relative"s to hospital. The man was blown-up like a big balloon. Sergeant Jiggy thought he had a germ of some sort. Well, they soon had him in the back of the truck and on his way to hospital to be treated. Sergeant Jiggy held on to him, as the driver negotiated the many different roads in and out of Trieste.

The Yugoslavs, before the new frontier came into being, would not allow a lorry full of grapes to leave a small village. The village was situated right on the border on the road to Gorizia. The lorry belonged to some local Italians. The deadline for the changeover was at midnight, so the Yugoslavs were not legally within their rights to stop it from moving from one place to another. The soldiers were there to keep the peace, but no one was sure what to do about the lorry full of grapes.

Early one evening a group of peasants, mainly women, came to the trattoria just over the border in Italy where the soldiers were stationed and petitioned Sergeant Jiggy. The peasants were very angry. They wanted to move their grapes over the border. The man who owned the trattoria had given the officer a room, and when the peasants heard about this they appealed to the owner in the hope that he could influence the officer.

When the Lieutenant appeared outside the trattoria the peasants spoke to him. Sergeant Jiggy understood their plight and translated what he could to the officer. Lieutenant Morrison"s first reaction was, "No, I"m afraid we can"t take part in this, sergeant, we have to stay neutral."

Sergeant Jiggy hardly needed to translate the foreign words to the Italian men and women beside him, but when he did the peasants got into a terrible state.

Sergeant Jiggy in the confusion, suggested, "We can still be neutral, sir. They are entitled to move their grapes," and he volunteered to escort the lorry over the border.

The Italians, by this time, were getting very agitated, for it was fast approaching the time for the new frontier to come into existence.

Lieutenant Morrison, after a great deal of thought, finally gave

Sergeant Jiggy permission to take a few men up to the village and see what they could do.

Presently, Sergeant Jiggy and half a dozen Guardsmen marched to the farmhouse where the lorry was stationed. They noticed some 10 or 12 Yugoslavs standing outside the farm, and when the Yugoslavs saw the peasants approach with the soldiers they started shouting insults, and threatening them.

When everything was eventually sorted out the peasants got on board and, with only minutes to go before the new frontier came into force, the lorry load of grapes arrived safely over the border onto Italian soil escorted by Sergeant Jiggy.

When they arrived over the border all the Italian woman, shouted, "Grazie Sergente!" for they were very pleased indeed to have beaten the deadline.

Sergeant Jiggy included this incident in his report to HQ:

Report on the handing over of the French Line to the Italians and Yugoslavs:

No 11 Platoon arrived at 08.45 at the trattoria which we decided 10 days ago would be our Pltn HQ. The trattoria was situated 400 metres from Road Post No. 121. No. 2 Section under the command of Lieutenant Stewart left us to take up their position on Road Post No 120. At 0900 hours a guard with L/Sgt McLafferty as Section Commander and consisting of one L/cpl and 6 Guardsmen took up position on 121 Road Post. They were marched from Platoon HQ by 2 Pipers. They were made more familiar with the orders and instructions: check all documents and licences of Automobiles going from Italy towards Yugoslavia as a precaution against theft.

Contact by this section was with field telephone and 38 set radio. At 0930 hours Lieutenant Stewart reported by 38 set radio that he had mounted his guard on R.P 120 and from 9.30 hours we were in constant contact with 120 & 121 Road Posts, also with Company HQ by phone. At 0930 hours the Italian Caribineri arrived at our Platoon HQ (6 soldiers under the command of A

Marishallo). We assisted them in every way possible and kept them up-to-date with the situation.

Many civilians were anxious to know details of the new frontier, and Lieutenant Morrison was kept busy explaining which villages in the immediate vicinity were to be in Yugoslavia or Italy. At midday Sunday everything was completely organized at platoon HQ and Lieutenant Morrison and myself had been to see our No. 120 Road Post.

At 1700 hours we were informed by Company HQ that ratification day had been postponed for 1 day.

All day Sunday many people were coming through the Road Post 121 from the area which was to come under Yugoslavia. Many pitiful sights were seen as people passed through with all their belongings on carts and lorries; some of this material was dumped just inside our area and then they went back home for more.

All the people from the little village of Canciani asked us to make certain if they would be under Yugoslavia. On our maps it showed the village just over the line and Lieutenant Morrisson checked up with HQ and was told that the village would definitely go to the Yugoslavs.

The peasants immediately started taking away all their belongings from their houses, also wood, grapes, etc.

The trattoria was a hive of activity, and at 1800 hours our 2 pipers played retreat in the square in front of the trattoria where all the civilians showed a lot of interest for the music and the kilts worn by the pipers.

At 2230 hours 3 civilian men reported to us that an unknown civilian had told all the civilians in the trattoria at Molinut that the Yugoslavs soldiers would definitely arrive that night in their new territory. We informed them that this was definitely untrue as American troops were still on the Morgan Line; however we sent patrols out in our area all night, but saw no trace of Yugoslav soldiers. There appears to have been a definite attempt by unknown civilians to create alarm during Sunday night, as the other civilians

182

reported similar incidents. Early this morning again we saw the Italians busy taking away all they could from the territory which was to be ceded to Yugoslavia.

Lieutenant Morrison and myself put in posts with notices in two languages on the area on each side of 121 Road Post. At 1400 hours a large truck with about 15 persons of both sexes came to platoon HQ and reported to us that they had been up at the village of Marchioli which is about 1.000 metres from 121 Road Post, and that Yugoslavs civilians had interfered with them as they were taking away the last of their goods which included grapes, and said that a man in the village had said that he would use a rifle against them if they took anymore away.

Lieutenant Morrison and myself accompanied these people back to the village where we found two Yugoslav families all standing around and looking rather menacing. The Italians commenced to get their goods on the trucks while the Yugoslavs made insulting remarks to them, example: "When the Yugoslav soldiers arrive tonight this will be a better place to live in!"

We noticed a Yugoslav flag flying in the village. Our presence probably helped and the Italians got their goods on the truck and we all left. It is perhaps worth noting that 2 VG (Venezia Guilo) police refused to go up and do what we had done: merely act as escort and see fair play.

Another batch of Italian soldiers arrived and camped beside our Road Post 121 and at 1900 hours they had a guard of 3 on the Road Post with our soldiers.

We were informed at 23.15 hours that the American troops were leaving immediately from their positions in front of us on the Morgan Line. Our Road Post was clearly marked at night with 2 paraffin lamps one clearly showing the notice of the provisional boundary.

Lieutenant Morrison was continually in contact with 120 Road Post by phone and radio.

We visited the Road Post regularly during the night and at 0515 when I went down with piper Miller, 3 Yugoslavs had just arrived. I could make out three other soldiers in the background with about 15 civilians. I arranged an appointment at 0900 (Tuesday morning) and immediately informed Lieutenant Morrison. Fires were seen all night on many of the hillsides. At exactly 0900 Lieutenant Morrison met the Italian representative and 2 Officers and a Lieutenant of the Yugoslav army. Lieutenant Morrison showed them the boundary and explained about the sticks we had put in the area on each side of the road.

The Italian representative accepted the frontier as correct, but the Yugoslavs after a discussion by themselves told us that the Road Post should be 400 meters deeper in to Italy. I was acting as interpreter. When I asked why they thought we were wrong one of them produced an old small scale map with a line drawn across, supposed to be the French line.

Lieutenant Morrison showed the photograph copy of the official map, and I explained to them about the difference in the scale of the maps and that everything was shown more clearly on our map.

They were still not convinced but when Lieutenant Morrison showed them the documents in 3 languages with all the details for the taking over they agreed to accept it meantime, but added that they would inform their HQ about the difference. The Yugoslav representatives then left.

At 1000 hours L/Sgt McLafferty informed us by phone that a Yugoslav officer wished to speak to us at Road Post 121, lieutenant Morrison and I went to meet them.

The Bar Milano, situated right in the middle of Trieste, had a good atmosphere at night. The locals would come and go there, and the soldiers were always made welcome at the bar.

One night two men from Naples appeared up at the cafe and set up a little recording studio inside the bar. However, the two men could not speak any English. Many soldiers wanted to record popular songs and send messages home to Blighty. So

Sergeant Jiggy, who could speak the lingo by this time, became an interpreter for the performers and for his trouble the two men from Naples gave him a free disk. Sergeant Jiggy, to the delight of everyone in the cafe that night, sang an Italian love song:

> *Bimba Ti voglio bene*
> *Tu sei il mio unico amor*
> *Sento nelle mie vene*
> *Come un grande Ardor*
> *Sto Creando una Canzone*
> *Questa canzone D"amor*
> *Sotto la luna*
> *Vicino a Te*
> *Fanciulla Bionda*
> *Ti Voglio amare*
> *Il Tuo bel viso*
> *Vorrei baciar*
> *Il paradiso*
> *Vorrei sognar*
> *Sotto la luna*
> *Solo con te*
> *Fanciulla bionda*
> *Sepre con Te*

One night around 10 o"clock, after saying goodnight to the owner of the Cafe Bar Milano, Sergeant Jiggy headed back to his quarters. He was up early the next day on guard and wanted to get to bed early.

As he walked smartly back down the Dominica Rossetti, towards the barracks, he noticed a crowd of Italians standing in the middle of the street. Suddenly someone spotted him, and shouted, "Sergente! Sergente! Presto! Presto! C"e` un soldato cattivo!"

Sergeant Jiggy looked at the crowd, then he quickly made his way towards them. In the middle of this crowd a Guardsman and a young girl were involved in a dispute over a big bottle of vino. Sergeant Jiggy recognized the man. The soldier as soon as he set eyes on the sergeant stopped and the girl broke free. She stood there in tears holding the great big bottle of wine with both hands. The soldier had apparently been trying to take it from her.

Sergeant Jiggy ordered him to march up to the barracks; however just then an Italian man shouted after him, "I will go with you sergeant and give evidence against him," and the Guardsman"s fate was sealed.

The Guardsman was put into a single cell in the guardroom, and the incident was reported to the sergeant major. A few weeks later a court marshal took place, and the soldier was sentenced to detention. And it just so happened that Sergeant Jiggy got the job of taking the man up to Austria to a town called Lienz for the trial.

When the Guards were stationed in Pola a platoon had to stand by every day just in case of any trouble. One morning Sergeant Jiggy"s platoon was told to go down to a granary in the middle of the town. So this day he got his section together, and with their guns at the ready they raced down to the scene not knowing what to expect. However, when the arrived outside the building, they were supplied with batons and told to weed out any Yugoslavs hiding inside the store. Apparently the men inside were trying to steal the flower.

Sergeant Jiggy"s section started on the ground floor and worked their way up. The first men they came across were Yugoslavs and they arrested them. They sent them down the stairs to where the other soldiers were waiting, and there they were finally put into trucks. Sergeant Jiggy, a little later on, came across a man on the second floor hiding behind some large sacks. When the man saw Sergeant Jiggy approach him he popped his head up, and then in a relaxed manner came forward to speak to him.

Sergeant Jiggy showed him the baton in his hand, then he challenged him: "Who are you?" he said, in an angry tone.

Just before the man felt the truncheon over his head, he cried out in a Yankee voice, "No, no, no, Sergeant, I am an American intelligence officer, it is me who has been responsible for alerting your Company Commander about what has been going on here!"

The rest of the Yugoslavs, who were hiding in the granary, were soon weeded out, arrested, and then taken away to jail.

On the day Field Marshal Alexander closed his headquarters at Caserta, Sergeant Jiggy"s section was part of the Guard Of Honour. The Guards left early that morning by train and arrived at the lovely town of Caserta in plenty of time. It was a big parade. The Scots Guards were formed up next to an American battalion. The Guards had brought the pipe band down with them, and they made quite an impression.

Sunday, 9 September, 1945: At Searchlight Tattoo. Field Marshal Alexander was there.

On the day they closed the Allied Field Headquarters in Italy, the heat became almost unbearable, and quite a few American soldiers fainted. Among the high-ranking officials who witnessed the end of the Allies in Italy was the Italian Prime Minister Signor De Gasperi.

16

On the same day, 10 February 1947, as Field Marshal Kettering pleaded not guilty to war crimes, Sergeant Jiggy, from his quarters two stories up, watched the piper and eight Guardsmen march towards the barracks in Trieste. The majority of the people in Trieste, just like the sergeant, liked to watch the soldiers parade through the streets. The soldiers at that moment were beating retreat back to the regimental building in the Domenica Rossetti.

The Sergeant gazed towards the main entrance of the barracks, then he looked out over the modern town of Trieste. The tower blocks and the houses directly in front of him, around early evening, seemed to symbolize a peaceful world inside a town full of paradoxes. Behind the buildings lay the picturesque street the Viale XX Settembre, built in the time of Emperor Franz 1, and as his eye followed the line of trees, he thought about all the times he had walked up and down that idyllic street, by the cafe-bars, shops and restaurants. Then he looked left over towards the harbour, in the direction of Stazione Marittima, then over in the direction of the Ospedale Maggiore, the Piazza della Borsa, and then finally towards the Piazza del Unita.

Trieste had a long history, and sometimes when you were high up you could sense the past as you glanced here and there from the old to the new buildings. The Romans had been here around 33 BC; Barbarians, Ostrogoths, Byzantines, Franks, and many others had followed on from them. The Venetians took Trieste in 1508. When it became a free port the French used it as a fortress in 1813, then it was occupied by the victorious Austrians; after the First World War Trieste became Italian.

Sergeant Jiggy had been stationed here in Trieste for about two years now; he liked the city it was like a second home to him. Peacetime duties for the men of the Scots Guards, who were living in Trieste just after the Second World War, were mostly spent polishing and cleaning equipment. Guard duties included: Brigade Headquarters, a prisoner of war camp, barrack guard, a guard at the Piazza dell"Unita, a guard at the Loyd Trestini Building, and at the Governor"s Palace.

As he polished his boots he thought about all the duties he had to perform next week; in fact, on reflection, every third day, he was on some sort of guard duty. The schedule was really hectic.

The sergeant, to break the humdrum existence of a peacetime soldier, wondered about the barracks that he lived in. He knew it had been built in the time of the Austria Hungarian Empire and, as he gazed down the beautiful treelined street, the Viale XX Settembre, once again, he thought about all the different soldiers who, in peacetime and in war, just like him, must have marched through this fine city up to the barracks. He knew that after the Italians, had come the Germans, then the Second Coldstream Guards, then the First Battalion Scots Guards. Now everyone in Trieste was asking the question: "Who will be next?"

That cold February evening, when Sergeant Jiggy was busy cleaning his boots, the Company Sergeant Major Thomson, known to everyone in the Battalion as "Big Spud," marched into his billet, and cried in a commanding voice, "Sergeant, I want you to go down and see R.S.M. Brown. He wants to see you, right away!"

A few moments later, in a small room filled with military books on the ground floor, not far from the guardroom, R.S.M.

Brown sitting at his desk gave the tall handsome Scotsman his orders: "Sergeant, I have a very important guard duty for you to carry out. I want you to take guard of a woman prisoner at the Jesuit women"s prison in Trieste. I"m at present getting your orders printed." He paused for a moment, then he continued, "Under no circumstance is she to speak to anyone without the direct permission from the Governor of Trieste, or our own Adjutant P.E.G. Balfour. Is that clear, sergeant?"

"Yes, sir!"

R.S.M George Brown stood up and as he walked around the room, he seemed to relax. Then he addressed the sergeant in a calm official tone, "This morning a woman shot Brigadier R.W.M De Winton, commander of the 13th British Infantry Brigade, in Pola - apparently it happened on the parade ground while he was inspecting the guard outside his headquarters."

The news was very sad indeed: for the brigadier, who had served in Palestine, France, North Africa, and Sicily, had lived through the war only to die at the hand of an assassin. The assassin fired three shots into the brigadier"s back. A private soldier had been apparently hit too, but it was not serious. The assassin after shooting the brigadier had dropped the automatic pistol, and was arrested.

The shooting, strangely enough, happened on the same day as the signing of the Peace Treaty in Trieste. Many Italians up and down Italy were angry at Great Britain for having given up the once proud Roman Citadel, Pola, to Yugoslavia. This act would surely be seen as revenge.

Sergeant Jiggy, when the orders came through, walked smartly down the stairs, and from a room inside the barracks he mobilized six Guardsmen and a corporal. When he stepped outside into the square he felt the chill of the night air. The evil force that starts wars and conflicts seemed to be on the go again. The death of an innocent man had brought the war back into focus.

Presently, the sergeant approached the 15-hundredweight truck parked outside the guardroom at the entrance to the barracks. Six Guardsmen and a corporal then all climbed inside the back of the vehicle.

Standing alone beside the vehicle Sergeant Jiggy checked his orders once again. Then he climbed into the front of the truck, and the escort headed for the prison. The prison was known to be run by nuns, and was situated somewhere in the city centre of Trieste.

Directly the six Guardsmen, the corporal, and the sergeant entered the Jesuit prison and lined up. After the sergeant had read out his orders, a Guardsman and a corporal followed him upstairs to where the assassin was being held. As they walked towards the single cell Sergeant Jiggy could see where the prisoner was being held: for the cell door was open. The rest of the soldiers stayed downstairs; they went into a spare room inside the prison and waited there.

When they reached the single cell the sergeant, the corporal, and the Guardsman all stood to attention in front of a large desk. The soldier on guard at the prison told Sergeant Jiggy: "Her name is Maria Pasquinelli, she is a young Italian woman."

The name of the woman, when spoken, seemed to change the whole atmosphere inside the women"s prison; and for a moment it was as if everything in this life, that had a name, had been decided a long time ago in some other age.

After a moment or two Sergeant Jiggy walked towards the entrance of the single dark cell, and from that single room three material objects impressed themselves upon his senses: a bed, a chair, and a forlorn figure standing in a red coat.

The common woman in the red coat heard the soldiers talking outside, she seemed to understand something as if from that other world where things are said but never heard. Then she heard the Sergeant"s voice say something to her in her own native tongue: "I am the sergeant of the guard. I will be here

191

until tomorrow to ten o"clock. Is there anything I can get you, madam?"

Maria Pasquinelli did not say anything; she turned away grief-stricken.

Sergeant Jiggy suddenly caught another image of her character, she seemed to him a country type. And after she had wandered back about two paces she turned round and looked at his face again.

Maria Pasquinelli seemed to be overcome by unbelievable events hovering back and forth from the future to the past, and from the past to the future. The woman in the red coat seemed to the soldier not to be able to quite understand the natural expressions in the present. This feeling he felt had made her tight-lipped and taciturn, and he felt that this was the reason she did not speak to him.

The shots that killed the brigadier must have fired again and again inside the assassin"s head that night, as she sat there inside the single cell of the Jesuit prison. She must have gone over the events time and time again. She must have thought about her past, her family, her friends, the dead brigadier, the nuns, and the soldiers who had come to guard her. She must have looked up at the crucifix upon the wall and wondered about everlasting life for those who have fallen. And on reflection after the major chord of her tangled thoughts had settled then disappeared again, she must have wondered what lay in store for her tomorrow.

The next day Maria Pasquinelli spoke to the sergeant, she told him in Italian, "Yesterday, I was so upset at what I had done that I could not speak." Then after looking at the sergeant"s face, and feeling that she could trust him, she added, "I was in charge of a committee who were taking their war dead back home to Italy by boat; we were going to dig up the graves, for we did not want our friends and relatives to be buried in Yugoslavia. I had gone to work there as a clerk for the

192

committee arranging the exodus of Italians from Pola."

The sergeant listened carefully and nodded. He knew that earlier that day the funeral of Brigadier De Winton had taken place at Udine at a British Military cemetery. Jonny Roe, the Scots Guards piper from Callender, had played the lament there. He had also heard that the Worcestershire Regiment band had played Chopin"s Funeral March, and that the troops of the Royal Sussex Regiment, the Essex Regiment, the King"s Royal Rifle Corps, and 6th Royal Tank Regiment, along with the Scots Guards, had all lined the route.

Maria Pasquinelli seemed pleased when Sergeant Jiggy"s face came on duty every third day. Maria did not speak to anyone else, for she knew the Scotsman could speak a little Italian.

On 13 February 1947, the Italian Prime Minister, Signor de Gasperi, told the Assembly, "The allied authorities were warned that Maria Pasquinelli had intended to murder a senior British officer." He added: "The allied authorities had been warned of the murderess"s intention therefore the Italian authorities cannot be blamed. The responsibility is that of the allies in Pola. Such episodes come from a feeling of exasperation against the peace treaty, but the Italian authorities had done everything possible to calm this agitation."

The London Times, 14 February 1947 carried a story: From Our Special Correspondent Trieste, that had some more information as regards the motive behind the shooting:

"Maria Pasquinelli the Italian school teacher who assassinated Brig De Winton commander of the British Garrison at Pola, on Monday has been transferred from Pola to Trieste. When arrested she was carrying a letter which is alleged to state that for many months she had planned to make a gesture at Pola, and had chosen February 10, 1947, as the most suitable day. Her gesture was intended as a protest against handing over the city, which she regarded as Italy"s "last outpost". She regarded the senior military officer, whoever he might be, as "the nearest representative of the big Four" who had betrayed her country. When arrested the woman showed not the slightest perturbation, and maintained a cynical attitude."

"From the director of the Pola exodus committee your Correspondent learned that Pasquinelli, who was born at Florence in 1913, had been employed as his secretary for about a week. Her request to work with the committee was approved because of her burning enthusiasm for the cause of Pola and Istria, and because she said she intended to study conditions on the spot and write a thesis, to obtain her degree, on the Slav drive westwards. Her offer to work as an unpaid volunteer was accepted and the woman proved herself and indefatigable assistant. In conversation she is said to have expressed deep resentment at the alleged failure of the allies to maintain their promises to Italy."

"Pasquinelli is described as a short dark, almost negroid type with crisp black hair and sturdy physique. After the armistice she is believed to have worked to promote Italian interests in Dalmatia, where she was arrested by the Yugoslavs. Later she succeeded in returning to Italy, where she had contacts with the partisan movement. She lived for a time at Trieste and Pola, but being suspected of underground collaboration with the Badoglio Government and the allies was arrested by the German S.S. and imprisoned at Trieste, whence she managed to escape."

"This report of her past, taken together with her remarkable composure during and since the shooting, has strengthened the impression that the woman had long been moving in fanatical nationalistic circles which may partly have inspired her. She apparently had sufficient private funds to maintain herself in a hotel at Pola."

When Sergeant Jiggy came back on duty she told him in a low voice, "I am glad to see you again."

The Sergeant, as he stood on guard, wondered about the woman who had rebelled against the peace treaty, and its unjust conditions. He knew that it had now been reported in the press that this woman, Maria Pasquinelli, willfully and with intent killed the Brigadier, because she was against pan-Slavism, and American Imperialism, "And yet an ordinary face I could have come across back home on a country road from Waterfoot to Eaglesham," he thought to himself.

Sergeant Jiggy was amazed when he heard that 5,000 Italians had already left Pola, and that 25,000 others were making preparations to leave; some of them had dug up their dead relatives so that they could take them back to Italy and bury them there. The place where Maria Pasquinelli had shot the brigadier was, by all accounts, now like a ghost town. All the traffic was now heading for the harbour or the train station.

One day, not long after the brigadier had been laid to rest, a big crowd of officers of all ranks appeared outside her cell: generals, colonels, majors, regimental sergeant majors, even the adjutant was there.

The R.S.M. after a moment or two walked over to Sergeant Jiggy and asked him about the conditions, as regards the prisoner.

Sergeant Jiggy replied, "Sir, this morning the prisoner gave me a note requesting clean underwear," after a short pause he felt he should add to this, "I feel it would be better, sir, if the nuns could deal with this request. The nuns as you know bring her food over to me."

The R.S.M. told the high ranking officers what the sergeant had said, and eventually after some discourse, among themselves, it was agreed that communication between the nuns and the prisoner could take place.

Maria Pasquinelli every morning and every afternoon got one

195

hour"s exercise in the courtyard. At lunch time this day a major and a sergeant appeared. They both stood in the doorway, and for a time watched the prisoner and Sergeant Jiggy outside in the exercise area.

The major suddenly, in a commanding voice, shouted, "Sergeant, bring that woman over here!"

Sergeant Jiggy knew his orders and he turned round and refused, "I am sorry, sir, I have strict orders from the Governor of Trieste: the prisoner has not to speak to anyone."

The major, very annoyed, tried again, "I am Major Armstrong, and I have to make arrangements for her trial."

Sergeant Jiggy refused to take Maria Pasquinelli over to him, "You will have to see Cpt Balfour at the Barracks, or the Governor of Trieste, if you want to get permission. Sir!"

The following day the man came back with written permission and then the wheels of justice were set in motion.

Time went by slowly and everything seemed to go on as normal, then just before her trial, very early in the morning around six o"clock, Maria Pasquinelli beckoned Sergeant Jiggy towards her. She wanted to speak to him. She said anxiously in a low voice: "I would like to go to chapel, sergeant; I want to see a priest. I want confession."

Sergeant Jiggy, aware of his orders and knowing the chapel to be downstairs, had to think long and hard about this request.

The following evening, 9 April 1947, Sergeant Jiggy in the Barracks heard that the trial had reopened, and that Major P. F. Malin R.A.M.C. senior officer of the psychiatrists" committee had pronounced Maria Pasquinelli mentally sane, but from the medical point of view of "limited responsibility." The President had reprimanded the defence saying that they were, "manipulating the written law of the land to suit its purposes." Feeling upset the Counsel of the defence shouted back at him. "I do not act as an ordinary lawyer, but as one Italian defending another." Several people in the gallery then shouted, "Long live

196

Italy," and hand clapping broke out among the public.

The following day, 10 April 1947, a report appeared in the London Times newspaper:

"The allied military court here found Maria Pasquinelli, 34 year old school teacher, Guilty of charges of having willfully, with intent and premeditation killed Brigadier R. W. M. De Winton D.S.O. The commander of the 13th British Infantry Brigade at Pola."

"When the hearing resumed this morning the defence submitted that there was no case against the accused who had acted in, "a state of necessity to avert imminent danger." Council said that the danger consisted of the prospect of the systematic racial suppression and extermination of Italians by Yugoslavs, in Pola and Istria, after the Italian peace treaty had entered into force. Pasquinelli believed that by Killing Brigadier De Winton she would draw the attention of the world to such a danger and avert it."

"After a short consultation the president announced that the court did not accept the thesis of the defence. The presumed danger would come to Italians from Yugoslavs, but the accused had killed a British subject. These circumstances decisively removed the existence of any "state of necessity"."

"The verdict of guilty was then pronounced, and the court adjourned till tomorrow afternoon."

The following day, 11 April 1947, Maria Pasquinelli was sentenced to death by an allied general court-martial for having assassinated the commander of the 13th Infantry Brigade at Pola. She was told that she could appeal within 30 days.

Pasquinelli exclaimed, "I shall not plead for mercy from the oppressors of my land!"

Some people, inside the court, shouted out loudly: "Bravo Maria!" before order was restored.

A few days later just before going to his bed Sergeant Jiggy picked up the British Forces daily paper, the Union Jack, and he read the heading on the front page, Pasquinelli Sentenced To Death. Then he read the story:

"Maria Pasquinelli Italian school teacher and assassin of Brig RWM De Winton, at Pola of February 10, was last night sentenced to death by a military tribunal at Trieste. Wild cheers rang through the closely-packed courtroom, as Pasquinelli, in a high, firm voice told the court that she had no intention of appealing against the sentence."

"Thank you for your courtesy," she said, "but I will not appeal to the oppressors of my native land."

"As she strode quickly from the room wearing a red coat she wore on the day of the shooting and escorted by two nuns who had been with her throughout the trial spectators cried, "Bravo!" Women among them began sobbing and one - believed to be Pasquinelli"s sister - became hysterical and had to be removed."

Sergeant Jiggy, in his billet that night, thought long and hard about the woman from Pola, and as he folded the paper and put it away - so that one day he may reflect upon it - he uttered to himself, "A most unusual guard, indeed."

17

Willie Keith, a Guardsman friend, while still in Italy wanted to go and see the Pope in St. Peter"s Square. So one Sunday he asked Sergeant Jiggy if he would go along with him. Sergeant Jiggy, although a Protestant, agreed to travel with him. He knew that religion had no sides to it when it came to Jesus. The two men, on the appointed day, arrived in good time for the Sunday service in the magnificent square.

The man up there on the balcony, Pope Pius X11, just like everyone else in Italy had had a terrible time of it during the Second World War. He had seen the rise of Fascism in his country. He had seen Allied troops and German troops fight a war on Italian soil. He had seen Italian towns and countries destroyed, thousands killed, maimed, and wounded. His position was similar to that of Pope Benedict XV: the First World War Pope used diplomacy when faced with aggression. However, the question of the Jews became a difficult one for Pius X11; for he was either for them or against them being thrown into concentration camps. Many people understood his position: why he did business with the Nazi party, and why he worked behind the scenes to help the Jews. However, many didn"t, and said that he had never uttered a word against Hitler"s mass extermination policy. Some people said that the man, who had once been a young Vatican lawyer, was terrified of communism, and this was why he acted the way he did.

On 23 January 1946 Sergeant Jiggy returned to Britain for a few days leave, and on his way back to the regiment at Trieste he stopped off at Calais. There at the station, as he was required to do, he read the noticeboard. As he stared at it he was surprised to see his name on a piece of paper up there on the board. The instruction beside his name read:

"Movement Order. No 198 Transit Camp. Serial No. 198/T, 23rd Jan 46: The under named personnel will proceed to 2 Br. C.R.U Villach by rail on 23rd January 1946, for onward routing as shown. Escort & Prisoner. Total Party 4 Other Ranks."

Inside a tent at Movement Control in France, Sergeant Jiggy was given further instructions. The man in charge of Movement Control told him: "You have to take charge of a prisoner, a Lancashire Fusilier, and see to it that he is returned to his regiment at Villach, Austria. The prisoner is a deserter, and has apparently committed many crimes in Italy."

Four other ranks were gathered together and they accompanied the sergeant to where the prisoner was being held; after the prisoner had been signed for, Sergeant Jiggy went to his cell. When the door opened the man in question stood up, he was around 5ft 6in, and handcuffs were duly put on him. Not long after this, around midday, the sergeant and his men, and the prisoner boarded a train that was going straight through to Villach. Inside the train the prisoner did not say very much. He just sat there looking out of the window.

However, the Lancashire Fusilier, when they got away from the built-up areas started to speak. After a few casual words about the war, he told them about what he had been up to. He said bluntly, "I deserted the regiment in Italy, and I got up as far as Milan and there I went into a jewellers" shop, for I was short of money. I said to the jeweller behind the desk, "Give me

200

some money or I"ll shoot you!" and I put the revolver on the table in front of him, to show him that I meant business. The jeweller refused to give me the money, so I shot him and helped myself to the cash and some other things in his shop. I managed to get as far as Calais, by jumping on lorries, trains and buses, but when I got to Calais I couldn"t get on board a boat to cross the channel; for I didn"t have one of those stupid boat passes. I hung around the bars and different places where the soldiers and sailors go, hoping to pick one up, but I couldn"t get a hold of one. The other morning when I was walking along towards the pier the Military Police suddenly appeared. They picked me up right away. I guess I looked the part: for I hadn"t shaved or washed for days. Then they threw me in the slammer at the station."

Sergeant Jiggy and other soldiers listened to him and no one really seemed surprised, for he had all the hallmarks of a deserter: bedraggled and unclean.

The desperado did not say if the jeweller died from his wounds or not, and after he had told his story the prisoner seemed to relax. Then he asked the sergeant if he could go to the toilet. When Sergeant Jiggy took him there he took the handcuffs off him, but he held the door ajar. He did not want him to disappear like the soldier on the train he had met just north of Rome: for he too had said that he was going for a piss, then vanished into thin air.

When they got to Villach they went to Movement Control. The Military Police were there waiting for them. They had transport at the ready. The Military Police drove the sergeant and his men, and the prisoner up into the mountains to where the Lancashire Fusiliers had their camp.

The R.S.M. must have been anxious to see the prisoner; for he had been sitting at his window by the courtyard for some time watching for the jeep. When it arrived and the prisoner got out of the jeep, the R.S.M. came running over to him, his hands held out as if to greet a holy man. In a state of high excitement, and pure theatre, as he got close to the prisoner, the R.S.M. waved and shouted: "Aha, they"ve got you at last - you"re back home!" and then he grabbed him.

The prisoner who had shot the jeweller in Milan was then led away, and put in a cell.

The R.S.M. was very kind to Sergeant Jiggy and the other soldiers; he saw to it that they got something to eat right away. Then he told them to stay the night and go back the next day to their regiment, for they were quite a bit off the beaten track.

Sergeant Jiggy, around this time, wrote a last letter in to the Forest Magazine, entitled, Stubborn Enemies Will Have To Be Conquered:

At the moment I find it very difficult to think of the things I expect from Civvy Street after the war; in fact the only thing that the end of the war will mean to me and to many others, is an end of fear. With the end of fear, I expect gradually to obtain my balance of mind which has been upset by Active Service conditions. Then I may be able to take more interest and perhaps help to tackle the problems that are sure to arise after the war.

Often in off duty spells in the Front Line I have discussed the problems of peace with my comrades. We have gone into lots of subjects, but we always end up with the unanimous opinion that the discomfort and danger that we have suffered during this war must not go for nothing. I am sure the politicians will do all they can to make the world a happier place in which we live and it is nice to see that efforts have already been made in that direction, although I know that putting the peace time world into shape will not be an easy job. Ancient and stubborn enemies will still have to be conquered, enemies such as poverty, disunity, prejudice, insecurity, and class distinction, but I am quite confident that they too can be conquered. If we can defeat the most ruthless war machine the world has ever seen surely we have the vision and genius to organize the peace.

New leaders will arise among us men with courage, faith, and a simple human dignity. I am certain that most of the young men in uniform today will be prepared to stand up for their rights in peace as they have done in war. Our comrades who have passed from our midst have not given their lives in vain.

I look forward to being a civilian and having freedom once again.

On 6 September 1947, Sergeant Jiggy writes home, to his mother and father, with some good news:

I write to you from Sesana, a small town just outside Trieste, I came here from the Road Posts away in the hills on the Morgan Line.

Well, I have some good news for you folks, we are all going to England very soon, perhaps within three weeks.

Whenever we hand over the new frontier to the Italian soldiers after ratification of the Peace Treaty we are all going to London. We move from here to a place near Udine called Palmanova, we were there about 2 months ago you may remember, I don"t know what I will do with my dog, I would like to bring him home for you father, but the army kennels are full up and will not receive any more, and I think it costs about £20 in a civilian kennel for about 6 months quarantine. I have been terribly busy lately, and I could not get away to go home on leave, the Scots Guards have had an awful lot of territory to look after, the Guardsmen got leave, but platoon sergeants have had to carry on, so I hope to get my 19 days added on to my disembarkation leave when we get to London. I sent you a parcel away yesterday, I registered in it that I had: 1 pair nylon stockings, 1 pair silk stockings, films for the camera, a singlet, underpants, 3 pairs socks, a cake of soap, and a tin of tobacco for making cigarettes also some papers which I want you to keep for me. I was away all day yesterday with the officers in a jeep, we were making arrangements for taking up our position on the new frontier when we move from here. I will explain it all to you when

I get home. My dog fairly likes going about in a jeep. If you haven"t sent the condition powders father, I don"t think you should bother sending them now as I will be in England in 3 or 4 weeks time unless something unforeseen happens.

I hope you are keeping well mother, I haven"t heard from you for a while.

Did Ian have a good leave and where has he got to now?

I bought material for making a costume or a suit, I will try and get it sent away soon.

I hope to be able to go down to Trieste tomorrow to say cheerio to my friends in the town. We are all very sorry to leave this place, it has been our second home for over two years. And so I will say cheerio; it is certain this time about us going to Britain, because they have started packing a lot of stuff. All my love and best wishes. Your loving son George XXXXXX

So at the beginning of October 1947 the Battalion made their way back home. They had been away for more than four years.

When Sergeant Jiggy marched into Palmanova station with Lupo he heard a voice shout at him, "Sergeant bring that dog over hear!"

The voice belonged to the Commanding Officer. Sergeant Jiggy marched over to him. He could see the Commanding Officer was standing with some other officers, not far from the checkpoint.

"I hope sergeant, you are not foolish enough to think that you can take that dog into England with you."

Sergeant Jiggy, not sure how to reply, looked down at his old friend Lupo. Then he said, "No sir. I"m going to take him to the quarantine kennels at the Hook of Holland."

The Commanding Officer for a time wondered about this, then he said, "Okay, sergeant, carry on."

However, when they were sitting in the compartment of the train another officer came up to Sergeant Jiggy and after some discussion he suggested to him that he would take the dog, "If you give me Lupo, I will look after him for you, and see that he is well fed at Brigade Headquarters."

So after thinking about all the options with much regret Sergeant Jiggy let his old friend go. Just before the train pulled out of the station he stood on the platform and said goodbye to Lupo. As he clapped Lupo for the last time he knew that he had been a loving and kind dog.

The Guardsmen left Italy in a brand new train, provided by the Italian government. They travelled up to the Hook of Holland, and there crossed the channel by boat. The sea was rough, but after they had crossed it they made there way from Harwich to London.

Saturday, 17 January 1948: *I took over as Acting C.S.M, H.Q Coy. as C.M.S. Lang is going on leave. D/Sgt in waiting.*

Wednesday, 28 January 1948: *Ian came down to visit me this morning.*

Monday, 16 February 1948: *The 1st Battalion Scots Guards broke up today I was sent to L company. It was a sad day and we are all sorry that it has happened.*

Friday, 20 February 1948: *I done Picquet tonight; it began to snow.*

Thursday, 26 February 1948: At 08.30 was on Practise Parade as I am detailed to be Sergeant In Command at Widsor Castle on Monday (went to dance at Guildford).

The following month was quite busy too; it kicked off with a course at No. 3 Army College at Chisledon near Swindon, and not long after this a foreign language course.

Monday, 1 March 1948: *March Left Pirbright at 10.00hrs to go on a pre demob course at No. 3 army college at Chisledon, Nr Swindon.*

Thursday, 18 March 1948: We were taken to see an Italian Film, Erico 1V, at the academy.

At the end of April, Sergeant Jiggy received an invitation to the Coldstream Guards" Ball on St. George"s Day. However, there would be no Easter leave, for he was to be on Royal Guard Duty at Windsor Castle as senior sergeant.

On the great day the Royal Guard travelled in trucks up to Windsor Barracks, and there they mounted a guard. Presently, they marched behind the two bands: the Scots Guards Pipe Band and the Big Brass Band of the Grenadier Guards. The sun was shining; it was a lovely day. Sergeant Jiggy marched right up into the Windsor castle area, in front of the quadrangle where the old guard was standing waiting.

During the proceedings, while the sentries were being changed, he noticed out of the corner of his eye the King and Queen and the little princesses up on the balcony watching the changeover. This was a tremendous honour indeed for the man born on the south side of Glasgow.

Tuesday, 20 April 1948: *I was senior sergeant of the Windsor Castle Guard today. The Royal family are in residence.*

That day Sergeant Jiggy wondered why two Guardsmen wanted to go on a certain guard; it was only later on he found out that there was a kitchen round that side of the castle where they could get a friendly cup of tea.

In the evening the officer came to Sergeant Jiggy, and he said to him: "I have been invited to dinner with his majesty. I will leave you in charge, sergeant, but don"t forget to phone me if anything happens - there is a telephone in my room - and I will come back down right away."

So for a time Sergeant Jiggy was left in charge of the Windsor Castle Guard, while the platoon commander and guard commander were having dinner with the King and Queen, Princess Elizabeth, and Princess Margaret. Sergeant Jiggy in fact could hear the music being played by a small band of Grenadier Guardsmen, as they had their meal. At two o"clock in the morning Sergeant Jiggy and the officer walked round Windsor Castle and checked that everything was all right.

A few weeks later, when Sergeant Jiggy had finished his in-waiting, he wrote another letter home:

It is 1.30 am Thursday morning as I write from Windsor castle Guardroom, as a matter of fact I have just returned from a patrol of all the sentry posts.

I finished Sgt in-Waiting on Tuesday at 10.30 and I mounted on Windsor Castle Guard on Wednesday at 8.30am. It is not such a big guard now that the Royal Family have gone, there is 2 sergeants and 2 corporals and 16 men on here. The sentries get posted every two hours and we patrol the sentry posts in between times to make sure that all is well, and in case a sentry feels sick.

We are here for two days and so it will be Friday morning before we finish.

It is quite a good guard I have a telephone here, I wish you had a phone at home and I could phone you. I have my camera on guard with me, I will try and take some photographs. I saw a lot of tourists this morning looking round the castle.

Our pipe band marched us down from Victoria barracks in Windsor to the castle. I hope you are both keeping well, also Ian. Has Ian found a job yet?

I am going to send my wooden box home, one of the driver"s is going to take it to Brookwood Station, but I don"t think I will get it away this week. All the Guardsmen at Pirbright have got the peacetime uniform, but I won"t get it.

I was speaking to a sergeant major in the Mess at the weekend, he used to be with our Battalion and is now at Regimental HQ in London. He told me that I should go there and see if they can get me a job.

I am enclosing a duplicate copy of my Guard report that time I was here with the big guard. It will do for my collection of souvenirs, Ian will be able to explain it to you. I expect it will be 22nd or 23rd of May when I get demobbed. That is all for now cheerio, and best wishes all my love. Your loving son George XXX

When Sergeant Jiggy arrived at Central Station, Glasgow, 2 September, 1948, he walked from the platform carrying his kit bag. Not far from the ticket barrier a porter approached him and said politely, "Would you like me to carry your bag, sir?"

Sergeant Jiggy looked at his kit bag over his shoulder, then he looked at the porter, "I"ve carried this all the way from Italy; I think I can carry it the rest of the way," and he laughed.

He then walked down to the bus stop at Clyde Street and after a few minutes an Eaglesham bus appeared. The journey home was strange and wonderful. Was he really going home for good this time?

When he got to Clarkston about 30 minutes later the bus pulled in at the toll, just opposite the place where he had been born. Sergeant Jiggy looked across at the old house, Rowallandale. Just then a woman from the local area got on the bus. She was carrying some messages, and once safely on the conductor rang the bell and the bus moved off again.

Two stops later when Sergeant Jiggy got up to get off he noticed that the woman sitting there on the seat near the door was his mother. He smiled at her and when she noticed him she stood up and he kissed her. Sergeant Jiggy was home for good.